POSTCARDS 1

Brian Abbs
Chris Barker
Ingrid Freebairn

with **Stella Reilly**

Longman

longman.com

Postcards 1

Pearson Education, 10 Bank Street, White Plains, NY 10606

Vice president, director of publishing: Allen Ascher
Editorial director: Ed Lamprich
Publisher: Sherri Arbogast
Senior development editor: Stella Reilly
Development editors: Eliza Jensen, Tunde Dewey
Vice president, director of design and production: Rhea Banker
Executive managing editor: Linda Moser
Production manager: Liza Pleva
Associate managing editor: Mike Kemper
Director of manufacturing: Patrice Fraccio
Senior manufacturing buyer: Dave Dickey
Photo research: Aerin Csigay
Cover design: Ann France
Text design: Ann France and Pearson Education Development Group
Text composition: Pearson Education Development Group

This book was set in 11/14 palatino

ISBN: 0-13-092570-5

1 2 3 4 5 6 7 8 9 10–WC–07 06 05 04 03 02

Acknowledgments

The authors and publisher wish to acknowledge with gratitude the following reviewers, contributors, photographers and illustrators who helped in the development of *Postcards 1*:

Reviewers

Sônia de Almeida Bicudo, Brazil • **Angelita Moreno**, Brazil • **Celso dos Santos**, Brazil • **Marc Chevalier**, Chile • **Francisco Javier Arias**, Colombia • **Hernando Prada**, Colombia • **Claudia Amaya**, Colombia • **Juan Omar Valdez**, Dominican Republic • **JoAnn Miller**, Mexico • **María Cristina Merodio Tamés**, Mexico • **Blanca Jiménez**, Mexico • **Silvia Cecilia Angles Díaz**, Peru • **César Klauer**, Peru • **Maria Angélica Dafieno**, Peru • **Vanessa Elías Pastor**, Peru • **Clara Noela Cartaya de Herrero**, Venezuela • **Abigail Polivoda**, Venezuela

Contributors

Charles Green for writing the games, the projects, and the culture readings. • **David McKeegan** for writing the *"Let's Get Started."* unit • **Tunde Dewey** for writing the Progress Checks.

Illustration credits

pp. 2, 7, 8, 16, 22, 24, 25, 27, 28, 52, 56, 60 (col.1), 63 (col.2), 64 (col.2), 71, 78 (middle col. 1&2), 82, 95, 96, 97 Mike Hortens; pp. 3 (top), 69 Anna Veltfort; p. 3 (bottom 6A-F) Andrew Shiff; pp. 12 (top 4A-H, middle), 21 (col.1), 47 (top), 49 Brian Hughes; pp. 12 (bottom), 13, 50, 87 Robert Roper; pp. 68, 78 (top 10A-K) Peter Gunther; pp. 21 (col.2), 35 Tim Haggerty; pp. 30, 86 Don Dyen; pp.31, 59 Patrick Merrell; pp. 32, 61 (col.2), 91, 92 M. Teresa Aguilar; pp. 54, 76 Chris Reed; p. 58 Dan Clifford; pp. 60-61, 63(col.1) Hal Just; p. 64 (col.1A,B,D) Daniel Delvalle.

Text credits

p.30 "Absolutely Everybody." Words and music by A. Hicks, M. Holden, J. Ingram. ©1999 Dream Dealers Pty. Ltd., Mark Holden Songs, Transistor Music Australia Pty. Ltd. All rights reserved. Used by permission; p.45 Adapted from The Gap Generation by William Damon. USA Weekend magazine, April 27-29, 2001; p.58 "Hero." Words and music by Mariah Carey and Walter Afanasieff. Copyright ©1993 Sony/ATV Songs LLC, Rye Songs, WB Music Corp. and Wallyworld Music. This arrangement copyright ©2002 Sony/ATV Songs LLC, Rye Songs, WB Music Corp. and Wallyworld Music. All rights on behalf of Sony/ATV Songs LLC and Rye Songs administered by Sony/ATV Music Publishing, 8 Music Square West, Nashville, TN 37203. All rights on behalf of Wallyworld Music administered by WB Music Corp. International copyright secured. All rights reserved; p.73 Adapted from The Homework Ate My Family by Romesh Ratnesar. Time magazine, January 25, 1999; p.86 "Crazy for This Girl." Words and music by Jaron Lowenstein and Jeff Cohen. ©2000 EMI Blackwood Music Inc., TZITZIS What We Do Music and As You Wish Music. This arrangement ©2002 EMI Blackwood Music Inc., TZITZIS What We Do Music and As You Wish Music. All rights for TZITZIS What We Do Music controlled and Administered by EMI Blackwood Music Inc. All rights reserved. International copyright secured. Used by permission.

Photo credits

All original photography by Michal Heron; pp.4-5, 9, 10-11 (airport) Rodrigo Varela; pp.48-49 (theater) Abdiel Thorne; p.6: (1) Rufus F. Folkks/Corbis, (2) Reuters NewMedia Inc./Corbis, (3-5) AFP/Corbis, (6) Rufus F. Folkks/Corbis; p.7 Mitchell Gerber/Corbis; p. 8 (left and right) Tony Stone, (center) Telegraph public Library; p.14 (1) Rex Features, (2) Rob Lewine/ Corbis Stock Market, (3) Kit Kittle/Corbis, (4) p. Francoise Gervais/Corbis; pp.16-17 (center) Richard T. Nowitz/Corbis, (bottom) Hollenbeck Photography/International Stock; p.17 (top) Alan Schein/Corbis Stock Market, (center) Michael Newman/ PhotoEdit, (bottom left) Joseph Sohm/ ChromoSohm Inc./ Corbis , (bottom right) LWA/Dan Tardif/Corbis Stock Market; p.22 L. Clarke/Corbis; p. 26 (bottom) Pictor; p.30 Mark Allan/ Alpha/Globe Photos; p. 36 (left) AFP/Corbis, (center and right) Mitchell Gerber/Corbis; p.38 Glenn Campbell/Shooting Star ; pp.40-41 Neal Preston/ Corbis, p.40 (1-2) Reuters NewMedia Inc./ Corbis, (3) Azzara Steve/Corbis Sygma; p.41 (4) AFP/Corbis, (5) Reuters NewMedia Inc./Corbis, (6) AFP/Corbis; p.42 Glenn Campbell/Shooting Star; p.44 Jiang Jin/SuperStock; pp.44-45 SuperStock, Leland Bobbe/Corbis; p.53 (1) John & Dallas Heaton/Corbis, (2) Jim Scourletis/PictureQuest, (3) Kathy Ferguson-Johnson/PhotoEdit, (4) Steve Skjold/PhotoEdit; p. 55 Images; p. 58 AFP/Corbis ; p.70 Courtesy Microsoft Corporation; pp.72-73 (top) Tom Stewart/Corbis Stock Market, (center) Laura Dwight/PhotoEdit , (bottom) Ed Bock/Corbis Stock Market; p.73 Mug Shots/Corbis Stock Market; p.83 (A) Michael Newman/PhotoEdit, (B) Jon Feingersh/Corbis Stock Market, (C) Rob Lewine/Corbis Stock Market, (D) David Hiller/PhotoDisc/ Getty Images, (E) Jeff Zaruba/Corbis Stock Market, (F) Michael Keller/Corbis Stock Market, (G) Paul Barton/Corbis Stock Market, (H) LWA/Dan Tardif/Corbis Stock Market, (I) Mark Richards/PhotoEdit, (J) Bill Miles/Corbis Stock Market; p.84 (top) Pictor International/Picture Quest, (bottom) Ales Fevzer/ Corbis; p.86 Fitzroy Barrett/Globe Photos; p.93 (1) Richard Hutchings/PhotoEdit, (2) Charles Register/ PhotoQuest, (3) Mary Kate Denny/PhotoEdit, (4) AFP/Corbis; p.94 (1) LWA/ Dann Tardif/Corbis Stock Market, (2) Paul Barton/Corbis Stock Market, (3) Jose L. Palaez/Corbis Stock Market, (4) Lawrence Manning/Corbis; p.95 (1a-b) Craig Aurness/Corbis, (2) Courtesy of Simon Properties, (3a-b) Courtesy of Chipotle, (4a-b) Bill Aron/ PhotoEdit; p.98 (1) L. Clarke/Corbis; pp.98-99 (2) Australian Picture Library/Corbis; p.99 (3) Art on File/Corbis, (4) O. Alamany & E. Vicens/Corbis, (5) Paul A. Souders/Corbis, (6) Tom Brakefield/Corbis; p.100 (A) David Young-Wolff/PhotoEdit, (B) Ariel Skelley/Corbis Stock Market; pp.100-101 (C) Ariel Skelley/ Corbis Stock Market, (D) Philip Gould/Corbis; p.100 (A) Jade Albert Studios Inc./FPG/Getty Images.
Cover photos: Palms © Nik Wheeler/CORBIS; Teens © SW Productions/Getty Images; Miami © Joseph Sohm; ChromoSohm Inc./CORBIS; Soccer © TempSport/CORBIS; N'Sync © Ethan Miller/CORBIS; Macaw © Landing/Minden Pictures.

Contents

Scope and Sequence

Unit	Title	Communication	Grammar

1
Pages 4-9
	What's your name?	• Introduce oneself and others
		• Ask someone's name and age: *What? How old? Who?*
			• Subject pronouns
			• The verb *be*
			  – Affirmative statements
			  – Negative statements
			  – *Yes/No* questions

2 Pages 10-14	**This is Brian.**	• Introduce people • Ask where people and things are: *Where is/are* • Apologize and accept an apology	• Prepositions of location: *in, on, above, under, at* • Possessive adjectives
Page 15	**Progress Check 1 and 2**		
Pages 16-17	**Wide Angle 1:** From one country . . . to another		
3 Pages 18-23	**I'm Australian.**	• Talk about your nationality • Say where you are from	• Plurals of nouns: regular and irregular • *This/That*; *These/Those* • Articles: *a/an*
4 Pages 24-28	**What's your address?**	• Ask for and give names, addresses, and telephone numbers • Use *Can* to make a request and ask for clarification	• Information questions with *be* • Prepositions of time: *in, on*
Page 29	**Progress Check 3 and 4**		
Page 30	**Song 1:** Absolutely Everybody		
Page 31	**Game 1:** Heads or Tails		

5
Pages 32-37
	I have two sisters.	• Talk about your family
		• Ask what people look like
			• Possessives of nouns
			• Simple present tense: *have*
			  – Affirmative and negative statements
			  – *Any* in *Yes/No* questions and in negatives

6 Pages 38-42	**Do you like hip-hop music?**	• Talk about likes and dislikes • Ask what people look like • Describe people	• Simple present: *like* • Adjective position
Page 43	**Progress Check 5 and 6**		
Pages 44-45	**Wide Angle 2:** The Kids Are Alright		

Vocabulary	Skills	Learn to Learn	Pronunciation
Cardinal numbers	*Reading:* Read for specific information. *Speaking:* Talk about favorites. *Writing:* Write an informal letter.		Stress patterns of number pairs *thirteen/thirty*
Travel items	*Reading:* Read for specific information. *Writing:* Write questions. *Listening:* Listen for details.	Learning with a partner	/dʒ/ in *jam* vs. /y/ in *yam*
Cities Countries Nationalities	*Reading:* Take notes. *Speaking:* Ask questions about a reading. *Writing:* Write an informal letter.	Using capital letters	/ð/ in *there* vs. /d/ in *dare*
Ordinal numbers Months of the year	*Reading:* Scan a text for information. *Listening:* Listen for specific information.	Asking for clarification	/θ/ in *fourth* vs. /t/ in *fort*
Family members Hair and eye colors	*Reading:* Find specific information in a text. *Listening:* Take notes while listening. *Speaking:* Ask questions to get specific information.		Intonation patterns in questions
Adjectives related to physical description	*Reading:* Interpret a family tree. *Writing:* Write sentences based on a pattern. *Speaking:* Repeat information heard.	Learning English outside the classroom	/ɑ/ in *hot* vs. /ɔ/ in *hall*

Vocabulary	Skills	Learn to Learn	Pronunciation
Clock times United States currency	*Reading:* Infer meaning. *Listening:* Listen for specific information; listen for implied meaning.		/æ/ in *can* vs. /ɑ/ in *car*
Daily activities	*Reading:* Interpret a graph. *Listening:* Listen for specific information. *Writing:* Write a paragraph. *Speaking:* Interview classmates.		Final /s/, /z/, /ɪz/ sounds
Places in town Leisure-time activities	*Reading:* Read a map. *Listening:* Listen for specific information. *Speaking:* Ask questions to get information. *Writing:* Write a descriptive list in discourse form.	Reading the newspaper	
Rooms and parts of the house	*Reading:* Guess meaning from content. *Listening:* Listen to telephone messages. *Writing:* Fill in missing information.	Increasing your vocabulary	
Past-time markers Common party and fast foods	*Reading:* Read a text and identify pronoun referents. *Listening:* Listen to a phone message to get information.		
Some occupations	*Reading:* Read for specific information. *Speaking:* Ask *Yes/No* questions in the simple past.		Final sounds /t/, /d/, /ɪd/

Joey

Brian

Annie

Liza

Andy

Robbie Caroline

Let's get started.

1 The alphabet

A. 🎧 Listen and repeat the letters of the alphabet.

Aa Bb Cc Dd Ee Ff Gg Hh Ii
Jj Kk Ll Mm Nn Oo Pp Qq Rr
Ss Tt Uu Vv Ww Xx Yy Zz

B. 🎧 Listen again and circle the letters that you hear.

2 Colors

A. 🎧 Write the number next to the correct color. Then listen and repeat.

1. red	2. brown	3. blue
4. black	5. green	6. white
7. yellow	8. orange	

_5_   ___   ___   ___

___   ___   ___   ___

B. Look at the alphabet in Exercise 1. The consonants are green. The vowels are red.

Write the vowels: __*a*__ ___ ___ ___ ___

3 Numbers 1–20

A. 🎧 Listen and repeat the numbers.

1 one	8 eight	15 fifteen
2 two	9 nine	16 sixteen
3 three	10 ten	17 seventeen
4 four	11 eleven	18 eighteen
5 five	12 twelve	19 nineteen
6 six	13 thirteen	20 twenty
7 seven	14 fourteen	

B. Work with a partner. Take turns saying and spelling numbers.

A: Nine.
B: N-I-N-E.

4 Days of the week

A. 🎧 Listen and repeat the days of the week.

Sunday	Monday	Tuesday	Wednesday	Thursday	Friday	Saturday
			1	2	3	4

B. Now write the days into the puzzle. One day is missing!

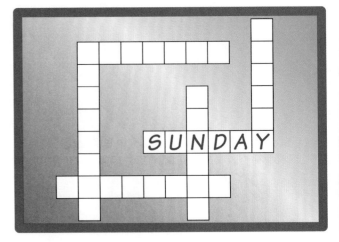

Write the missing day here: _____

5 Classroom objects

A. Look at the pictures in the grid and complete the chart below.

Object	Number/Letter	Color
board	1 D	black
book	_____	_____
chair	_____	_____
desk	_____	_____
notebook	_____	_____
pen	_____	_____
pencil	_____	_____
ruler	_____	_____

B. With a partner, sit face to face. Take turns guessing the objects in the grids.

A: 2C.
B: Desk.

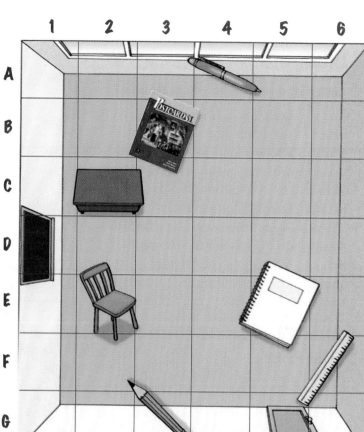

6 Classroom commands

Match the commands with the pictures.

1. Stand up. __D__

2. Write. _____

3. Sit down. _____

4. Listen. _____

5. Close your book. _____

6. Open your book. _____

1

What's your name?

Learning Goals

Communication
Introduce yourself and others
Ask someone's name and age:
What? How old?
Talk about favorites: *Who? What?*

Grammar
Subject pronouns
Simple present tense: *be*

Vocabulary
Cardinal numbers: 21–100

1 Dialogue

🎧 **Listen and read. How old is Robbie?**

Andy: Excuse me. Are you Brian Williams?
Brian: Yes, I am. Are you the Gibsons?
Andy: Yes, we are. I'm Andy—Andy Gibson. This is my sister, Liza.
Liza: Hello. Welcome to Miami, Brian.
Brian: Thanks! Are your parents here, too?
Robbie: My mom's here. She's outside.
Andy: Brian, this is my little brother.
Brian: Hi. What's your name?
Robbie: Robbie. And I'm not little! I'm six.
Brian: Nice to meet you, Robbie.
Robbie: How old are you, Brian?
Brian: I'm fifteen.
Robbie: Fifty!
Andy: No, not fifty, Robbie. Fifteen.

2 Comprehension

A. Write the names of the people in the boxes.

B. Write the information.

<u>Brian Williams</u> 1. The Gibson family's visitor

_____ 2. The sister's name

_____ 3. The name of the little brother

_____ 4. Brian's age

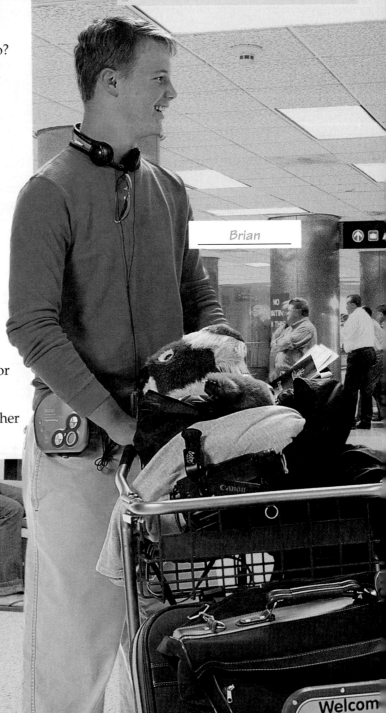

Brian

3 Vocabulary

Cardinal numbers: 21–100

🎧 Listen and repeat the numbers.

21 twenty-one	**30** thirty	**80** eighty
22 twenty-two	**40** forty	**90** ninety
23 twenty-three	**50** fifty	**100** one hundred
24 twenty-four	**60** sixty	
25 twenty-five	**70** seventy	

4 Pronunciation

A. 🎧 **Listen and repeat the numbers.**

12/20	16/60
13/30	17/70
14/40	18/80
15/50	19/90

B. 🎧 **Listen to a description of the Brown family. Circle the number you hear.**

1. 15   50
2. 13   30
3. 18   80
4. 19   90

GRAMMAR FOCUS

Simple present tense of *be*/Subject pronouns

Affirmative statements			Negative statements			
I	**am**	15 years old.	I	am	**not**	15 years old.
He			He			
She	**is**	15 years old.	She	is	**not**	15 years old.
It			It			
We			We			
You	**are**	15 years old.	You	are	**not**	15 years old.
They			They			

Long form		Short form
I am	→	**I'm**
He is	→	**He's**
She is	→	**She's**
It is	→	**It's**
We are	→	**We're**
You are	→	**You're**
They are	→	**They're**

5 Practice

Write the short forms (contractions).

1. (*You are*) ___You're___ my friend.

2. (*I am*) _____ 12 years old.

3. (*She is*) _____ my classmate.

4. (*He is*) _____ 40 years old.

5. (*They are*) _____ pen pals.

6. (*It is*) _____ my English homework.

6 Practice

Work with a partner. Identify the people in the pictures. Write sentences using contractions.

Tom Cruise	Shakira
Julia Roberts	Jackie Chan
98 Degrees	Jennifer Lopez

1. *She's Julia Roberts.* _____
2. _____
3. _____
4. _____
5. _____
6. _____

GRAMMAR FOCUS

Simple present tense of *be*

Yes/No questions	Affirmative answers	Negative answers
Am I OK?	Yes, you **are**.	No, **you're** not. (No, you **aren't**.)
Are you OK?	Yes, I **am**.	No, **I'm** not. (No, I **am not**.)
Is { he / she / it } OK?	Yes, { he / she / it } **is**.	No, **he's** not. (No, he **isn't**.)
		No, **she's** not. (No, she **isn't**.)
		No, **it's** not. (No, it **isn't**.)
Are { we / they } OK?	Yes, { we / they } **are**.	No, **we're** not. (No, we **aren't**.)
		No, **they're** not. (No, they **aren't**.)

7 Practice

Unscramble the words and write questions.
Then answer the questions.

1. you/Are/student/a
   Q: *Are you a student?*
   A: *Yes, I am.*

2. today/at school/your friends/Are
   Q: *Are your friends at school today?*
   A: _____

3. you/years/Are/old/10
   Q: _____
   A: _____

4. your English teacher/Is/American
   Q: _____
   A: _____

8 Communication

A. ⌒ **Listen to the dialogues.**

1. A: Hi. Are you Tim Benson?
   B: Yes, I am. I'm Tim Benson.
   A: Hello, Tim. I'm Maria Garcia.
2. A: Excuse me. Are you Sue Stevens?
   B: No, I'm not. I'm Jane Carlson.

**B. Role-play the dialogues with a partner.
Replace the names as shown.**

1. Tim Benson → Brad Pitt
   Maria Garcia → Your name
2. Sue Stevens → Jennifer Aniston
   Jane Carlson → Your name

9 Your Turn

Work with a partner. Ask each other these
questions and answer them.

What's your name?
How old are you?
What's your favorite movie?
Who's your favorite movie star?

10 Listening

⌒ **Listen. Rank the names of the top actors
according to the survey.**

Harrison Ford	Josh Hartnett
Russell Crowe	Tom Cruise

The Top Three Hollywood Actors

Number 1 _____
Number 2 _____
Number 3 _____

Pen Pals Wanted

Hi. My name's Elena. I'm from Guadalajara, Mexico. I'm 13. My favorite actor is Will Smith, and my favorite movie is *Harry Potter and the Sorcerer's Stone*. How about you? What's your favorite movie? Write to:
Elena Cruz, Box 218

Hello. I'm Trisha. I'm from Miami. I'm 12. I like Cameron Diaz. She's beautiful. My favorite movie is *Shrek*. Tell me about your favorites. Write to:
Trisha Blair, Box 749

Hi, there. I'm Tommy from New York. I'm 14. My favorite actor is Harrison Ford. He's really good! My favorite movies are the *Indiana Jones* movies. They're exciting. Write to me, OK? Write to:
Tommy Peterson, Box 356

11 Reading

Read the Pen Pal advertisements. Then fill in the chart.

	Elena	Trisha	Tommy	You
Age	13			
Last name	Cruz			
City	Guadalajara			
Favorite actor	Will Smith			
Favorite movie	Harry Potter			
Box number	218			

12 Speaking

Work with a partner. Talk about your favorite movies.

A: What's your favorite movie?
B: *The Lord of the Rings*. It's a great movie! What's your favorite movie?

13 Writing

Write about yourself and your favorites in your notebook. If you are interested, you can write to a pen pal on *http://www.epals.com*.

At the Airport

🎧 First, write the missing sentences. Choose from the box below. Then listen and check your work.

Who's your favorite, Liza?	Who's your favorite singer?	Thanks!
How old are you?	Yes, I am.	She's great.

1
Liza, are you in the same school as Andy?
(1) _____ He's in ninth grade. I'm in eighth.

2
(2) _____
I'm 14.
Yeah, she's old.

3
Robbie, look! Here's a present for you.
Wow! This is great!
(3) _____

4
Hey, Brian.
(4) _____
My favorite singer? Well, it's a music group. Destiny's Child.

5
(5) _____
Britney Spears.
(6) _____
Eww! Britney Spears! Yuck! My favorite is Usher.

6
(Whispering) So, Liza. Is Brian good-looking?

2 This is Brian.

1 Dialogue

🎧 **Listen and read. Circle another word for *luggage*.**

Robbie: There's my mom.
Brian: Where's your father?
Robbie: He's at home.
Andy: Mom, this is Brian.
Mom: Nice to meet you, Brian. How are you?
Brian: I'm fine, thanks.
Mom: Good. Kids, help Brian with his luggage. Where are your bags, Brian?
Brian: They're on the cart over there.
Andy: Brian, where's your video camera?
Brian: It's in my backpack. Oh, no! Where's my backpack? My passport is in there.
Liza: It's here, Brian, under your jacket.

(Later, at the Gibson's home.)

Robbie: Hey, Brian. Let's go to the beach today.
Liza: Robbie, we're busy.
Robbie: No, we're not.
Andy: Stop it, you two! Let's go inside, Brian.

2 Comprehension

Work with a partner. Write *True* or *False*. Correct the false statements.

1. Brian's bags are on the ground.
   False. They're on the cart.

2. The video camera is in the backpack.
   _____

3. The passport is in the jacket.
   _____

4. Mr. Gibson is at work.
   _____

5. Mrs. Gibson is at the airport.
   _____

3 Useful Phrases

A. 🎧 **Listen and repeat.**

- How are you?
- Nice to meet you.
- I'm fine, thank you./Fine, thanks.
- Let's go.

**B. Introduce a friend to your teacher.
Follow the example.**

Anthony:	Mrs. Roberts, this is Monica.
Mrs. Roberts:	Nice to meet you, Monica. How are you?
Monica:	Fine, thanks.

4 Vocabulary

Travel items

🎧 **Listen and repeat.**
Then match the words with the pictures.

1. backpack _D_
2. passport ____
3. jacket ____
4. luggage/bags ____
5. ticket ____
6. video camera ____
7. CD player ____
8. sunglasses ____

GRAMMAR FOCUS

Prepositions: *in, on, above, under, at*

Where are the CDs?

They're **in** the bag.
They're **on** the bag.

Where's the backpack?

It's **under** the table.
It's **above** the table.

Remember! Say *at* work; *at* home; *at* school.

---

5 Practice

A. Fill in the blanks with *in, on, under,* and *above.*

1. The CD player is ___under___ the bed.
2. The jacket is _____ the computer.
3. The video camera is _____ the bed.
4. The pencils are _____ the sneaker.
5. The backpack and the video games are _____ the floor.
6. The books are _____ the chair.

B. Work with a partner. Ask where things are in the picture.

A: Where are the sneakers?
B: They're on the chair.

6 Practice

Have a competition! Go to page 88.

GRAMMAR FOCUS

Possessive adjectives

Subject form		Possessive form	
I	→	**my**	**My** book is on the desk.
you	→	**your**	**Your** book is on the desk.
he	→	**his**	**His** book is on the desk.
she	→	**her**	**Her** book is on the desk.
we	→	**our**	**Our** books are on the desk.
they	→	**their**	**Their** books are on the desk.

7 Practice

Fill in the blanks with possessive adjectives. Then check your work with a partner.

Robbie: Brian, can I show you (1) __my__ room?

Brian: Sure. Where's (2) _____ room?

Robbie: Here it is. Here's (3) _____ favorite baseball. It's from my best friend.

Brian: That's cool. Let's play baseball later. So where are the other rooms?

Robbie: Here's Liza's room. See the poster? That's (4) _____ favorite group, 'NSync. I don't like them.

Brian: Really? They're OK. Now, where's Andy's room?

Robbie: It's here. (5) _____ room is big. I can't go into (6) _____ room. He always says, "Knock first." I think this is (7) _____ room, too, Brian.

Brian: So this is our room. It's OK with me if you come into (8) _____ room sometimes, Robbie. I'll talk to Andy. Where's (9) _____ parents' room?

Robbie: See that big door? That's (10) _____ room. We can't go in there.

Brian: That's OK. Come on. Let's bring (11) _____ luggage up.

8 Pronunciation

The sounds /y/ and /dʒ/

A. ⌒ Listen and repeat.

you—Jude	yes—Jess	use—juice
your—joy	yet—jet	yellow—Jell-O

B. ⌒ Listen and repeat.

1. Lemon Jell-O is yellow.
2. Is the jet plane here yet?
3. Jess said, "Yes."

9 Reading

Look at Brian's pictures from home. Match each paragraph with a picture.

A __2__   B _____   C _____   D _____

(A) This is my mother. Her name is Lucille. And that's my father. His name is George. They're at home in Canberra, Australia.

(B) This is my little sister. Her name is Sandra, Sandy for short. She's 14. Here she is at school.

(C) This is my big sister, Louise. She's 18 years old. She's a ballet student. Here she is in her ballet class.

(D) This is my dog, Spice Girl. Notice the koala bear on her back? That's Spice Girl's best friend, Nikki. They're in the backyard.

10 Writing

Work with a partner. Write five questions about Brian's family in your notebook. Use *who* and *where*. Then ask and answer your questions orally.

11 Listening

🎧 **Listen. Circle the correct answer.**

1. The family is
   (a) at the park.   (b) at home.   (c) at a restaurant.
2. Liza is
   (a) at the computer.   (b) in the kitchen.   (c) on the phone.
3. Brian and Andy are
   (a) in the bedroom.   (b) at the park.   (c) at the library.
4. Robbie is
   (a) in his room.   (b) in the kitchen.   (c) on the phone.

Learn to Learn

Working with a learning partner

In this unit, you did some exercises with a partner. Having a learning partner makes studying a new language easier and fun. For example, you can listen to songs in English together. You can practice dialogues together, learn new words together, or e-mail each other in English.

Progress Check *Units 1 and 2*

Grammar

A. Write the short forms (contractions). (1 point each)

1. (*He is*) ___He's___ my brother.
2. (*I am*) _____ hungry.
3. (*You are*) _____ here.
4. (*She is*) _____ his sister.
5. (*They are*) _____ students.
6. (*We are*) _____ at the beach.

B. Give true answers. (3 points each)

1. Are you American? *No, I'm not.* _____
2. Are you at school? _____
3. Is it Monday today? _____
4. Are your parents at home? _____
5. Is your best friend a student? _____

C. Fill in the blanks with possessive adjectives. (2 points each)

1. That's my brother's car. ___His___ car is big.
2. She's my mother. _____ name is Alicia.
3. They're our teachers. _____ names are Mr. Mendez and Ms. Torrez.
4. This is _____ city. We love it.
5. _____ father is in Asia. I miss him.

D. Fill in the blanks with *at, in, on, above,* or *under.* Use each preposition only once. (2 points each)

1. My mother is ___at___ home.
2. My pen is _____ the drawer.
3. The book is _____ the shelf.
4. The posters are on the wall _____ the bed.
5. My shoes are _____ the table.

E. Complete the sentences with *Who? Where? How?* or *What?* (2 points each)

1. A: ___What___'s your name?
   B: _____ old are you?
2. A: _____ are you?
   B: Fine, thanks.
3. A: _____'s that?
   B: That's Jennifer Lopez.
4. A: _____'s that?
   B: It's a video camera.
5. A: _____'s your mom?
   B: She's in the car.

Vocabulary

F. Write four words, phrases, or sentences for each of the categories below. Go to pages 2–3 to find the answers.

Days of the week	Classroom objects	Colors
Sunday	pencil	red

Communication

G. Work with a partner. Ask each other these questions. (3 points each)

1. What's your name?
2. How are you?
3. How old are you?
4. Where's your English book?
5. Are you 15 years old?

1 Reading

A. Read about Sonia and Armando. Where are they from? Circle the answers.

B. You and your partner are going to interview Sonia and Armando for your school paper. Ask each student three questions.

Questions for Sonia:

1. *How old are you?* _____
2. _____
3. _____

Questions for Armando:

1. _____
2. _____
3. _____

2 Listening

🎧 Listen to the interview. Then fill in the form for Leslie.

Interview Form

Name	Age
Country	First Language
Favorites	

3 Writing

Write a short paragraph about Leslie. Use the articles about Sonia and Armando as examples.

Leslie is 15 years old. She's from . . .

_____

4 Speaking

You are a new student. Choose a classmate who does not know you well. Introduce yourself to this classmate.

From One Country... to Another

1 **Sonia Zuge** is Brazilian. She's from Rio de Janeiro. Right now, her family lives in New York City. Sonia is in seventh grade.

"My name's Sonia Zuge. I'm 13. I'm a new student here. Right now, I am in two foreign-language classes: German and English. My favorite language is English. I like American and Latin music. My favorite singers are Christina Aguilera and Jessica Simpson."

2 **Armando Hernandez** is 15. He is from Mexico, but now he lives in Dallas, Texas. He is a dance student. He studies ballet and modern dance in Dallas. Armando is also in an English class. His first language is Spanish, and his second language is English.

"Hi. I'm Armando Hernandez. I'm 15 years old. My parents are in Mexico, but I'm here in the United States as a dance student. Right now, I'm a dancer with the Mexican Folklórico Company in Dallas."

3 I'm Australian.

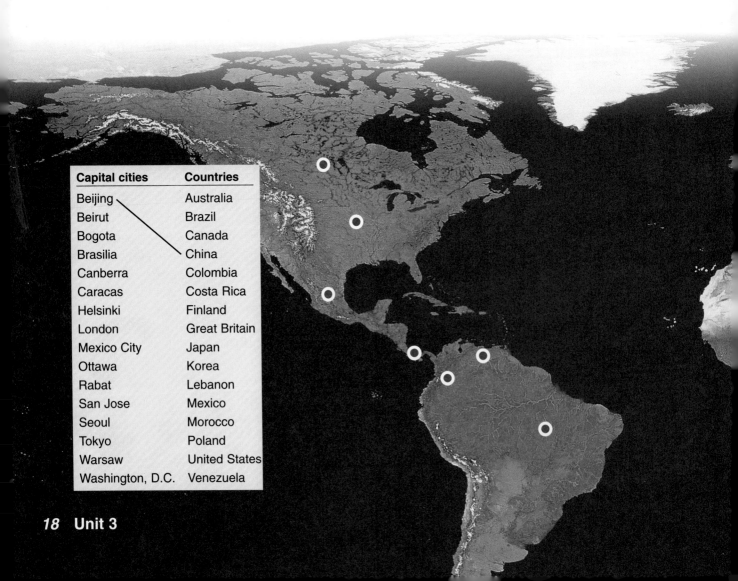

1 Vocabulary

Countries, capital cities, and nationalities

A. **Work with a partner. Match the capital cities and countries listed below. Then identify the countries marked with a ●.**

B. **Study the nationality endings on the right. Copy the countries from the chart below in your notebook. With a partner, write the nationality for each country.**

C. **🎧 Listen to the list and check your work in Exercise B. Then listen again and repeat.**

Learning Goals

Communication
Talk about your nationality and say where you are from
Apologize and accept an apology

Grammar
Plural of nouns
This/that; these/those
Articles: *a/an*

Vocabulary
Countries and nationalities

Country	Nationality
Australia	Austral**ian**
Canada	Canad**ian**
China	Chin**ese**
Finland	Finn**ish**
France	**French**

Capital cities	Countries
Beijing	Australia
Beirut	Brazil
Bogota	Canada
Brasilia	China
Canberra	Colombia
Caracas	Costa Rica
Helsinki	Finland
London	Great Britain
Mexico City	Japan
Ottawa	Korea
Rabat	Lebanon
San Jose	Mexico
Seoul	Morocco
Tokyo	Poland
Warsaw	United States
Washington, D.C.	Venezuela

2 Communication

Talking about where you are from

A. **Listen and repeat.**

A: Hi. What's your name?
B: Victoria.
A: Are you Spanish?
B: No, I'm not. I'm Mexican.
A: Where are you from?
B: I'm from Guadalajara.
    How about you?
A: I'm from England.

B. Work with a partner. You are from the United States and your partner is from a country in South America. Write a dialogue like Exercise A. Then role-play it.

GRAMMAR FOCUS

Plural of nouns

1. To most singular nouns, add **-s** or **-es**:
student	student**s**	bus	bus**es**
box	box**es**	beach	beach**es**
2. To nouns ending in a consonant and **-y**, add **-es** and change **y** to **i**:
city	cit**ies**	country	countr**ies**
3. To nouns ending in a vowel and **-y**, add **-s**:
boy	boy**s**	key	ke**ys**
4. Some irregular nouns:
man	**men**	child	**children**	woman	**women**
person	**people**	tooth	**teeth**	mouse	**mice**

3 Practice

A. Copy the words below in your notebook. Then write the plural forms.

1. person
2. girl
3. mouse
4. friend
5. fax
6. bus
7. woman
8. country
9. boy
10. kiss
11. dictionary
12. party
13. tooth
14. foot
15. child

B. Have a competition! Go to page 88.

4 Dialogue

A. Read the dialogue quickly. Circle the sentence that expresses an apology.

Andy: Hey, look out!
Eric: Oops, I'm sorry.
Andy: That's OK. Liza, it's Eric!
Eric: Hi, guys. How are you doing?
Liza: Good. Those skates are cool, Eric.
Eric: Thanks. They're great for tricks.
Liza: Cool. By the way, Eric, this is Brian.
Eric: Nice to meet you, Brian. Are you a new student in our school?
Brian: Well, only for two months.
Eric: Oh, you're the exchange student. Where are you from?
Brian: I'm Australian. I'm from Canberra.
Eric: Australia. Hmm. Koalas and Nicole Kidman. I'm kidding. Australia's cool. Well, I have to go. See you in school, Brian.
Brian: OK. Bye.

B. ⌒ Read the dialogue again as you listen.

5 Comprehension

Write *True* or *False*. Correct the false statements.

False 1. Andy, Liza, Brian, and Eric are *at the beach* ~~at the park~~.

_____ 2. Brian is an exchange student in Miami.

_____ 3. Liza likes Eric's skates.

_____ 4. Nicole Kidman is from Canada.

_____ 5. Canberra is in England.

6 Useful Phrases

A. ⌒ Listen and repeat.

- Look out!
- I have to go.
- See you. / Bye.
- That's OK.
- I'm sorry!

B. Choose one situation and write a dialogue. Use the expressions in Exercise A. Then role-play your dialogue.

- You are carrying hot chocolate. Someone is running toward you. Warn the person.
- You are on the phone with a classmate. Your mom needs you. End your conversation.

GRAMMAR FOCUS

This/That; These/Those

Singular

This is my book.   **That**'s your book.

Plural

These are my books.   **Those** are your books.

Articles *a* and *an*

What's this?   What's that?
It's **a v**ideo camera.   It's **an a**pple pie.

7 Pronunciation

The sounds /ð/ and /d/

A. 🎧 Listen and repeat.

/ð/	/d/
this	disk
there	dare
those	doze
that	dad

B. 🎧 Listen and repeat. Circle the words with the /ð/ sound.

1. This disk is broken.
2. These dishes are dirty.
3. Those students dozed in class.
4. That dog is theirs.

8 Practice

Look at the pictures. Fill in the blanks with *this*, *that*, *these*, and *those*.

1. Look at ___those___ red shoes.
2. I like _____ blue backpack.
3. _____ jacket is expensive!
4. Is _____ my wallet?
5. _____ pink cell phone is cool.
6. _____ umbrellas are from China.

9 Practice

A. Work with a partner. Find objects in your classroom. Ask each other the names of objects in English. Use *this*, *that*, *these*, and *those*.

A: What's this in English?
B: It's an eraser. What are those in English?
A: They're pencils.

B. Have a competition! Go to page 89.

10 Reading

A. Read the letter. As you read, underline the important information.

B. Compare your work with a classmate. Did you underline the same information? Discuss what kinds of information in the e-mail are important.

11 Speaking

Write three questions about Joy's letter. Choose a partner and take turns asking and answering your questions.

A: Is Joy Walsh American?
B: No, she's not. She's Canadian.
A: How old are the students in her class?

Dear fellow students,

My name is Joy Walsh. I'm 11 years old. I'm in sixth grade here in Alberta. Can you guess where Alberta is? It's in Canada.

My class wants to e-mail students in other countries. The kids in my class are 11 or 12 years old. We all like sports. Our favorite sports are hockey, skiing, and snowboarding. We also like movies and music.

If you want to write to my class, go to **http://www.epals.com.** In your e-mail, please tell us where you are from, your age, and your favorite things to do.

I hope to read your e-mail soon!

–Joy

C. Now, answer the questions in complete sentences.

1. What is the writer's name?

_____

2. Where is she from?

_____

3. What is her nationality?

_____

4. How old are the students in her class?

_____

5. What do they like?

_____

12 Writing

Work in groups of three. Write a letter to Joy. Share your letter with the class. With your teacher, go to *http://www.epals.com* and choose a class from one country to write to.

Learn to Learn

Using capital letters

Circle the capital letters in Joy's letter.
Discuss: When do you use capital letters?

At School

A. An exchange student is staying at your friend's house. What questions would you ask your friend about the student? Write the questions in your notebook. Do not read the dialogue yet.

B. 🎧 Now listen and read.

1. Hi, Annie.
   Hi, Liza. Hmm, you're happy.

2. Well, he's here! He's at my house.
   Who's here?
   The exchange student.

3. Oh? How old is he?
   He's 15.

4. Perfect. We're 14. Is he cute?
   Oh, Annie. He's really cute! His eyes are so blue!

5. Really? What's his name? Where's he from?
   Whoa! Don't get excited, Annie. His name's Brian. He's from Australia.

6. That's really perfect, Liza. I love Australians!
   And you love Canadians, too. And Americans. And . . .
   Ha-ha-ha. Very funny, Liza.

C. Read the dialogue again. Underline Annie's questions. Look at your questions. Do you have the same questions as Annie? What questions did you not ask?

4 What's your address?

Learning Goals

Communication
Ask for and give names, addresses, and telephone numbers
Make a request: *Can*
Ask for clarification

Grammar
Information questions with *be*
Prepositions of time: *in, on*

Vocabulary
Ordinal numbers
Months of the year

1 Dialogue

🎧 **Listen and read. Circle Brian's date of birth.**

Girl: Good morning. Can I help you?

Andy: Yes, please. Can my friend get a guest pass?

Girl: Sure. Let me get your information. What's your last name?

Brian: Williams.

Girl: Can you spell that, please?

Brian: Sure. It's W-I-L-L-I-A-M-S.

Girl: Williams. And your first name?

Brian: It's Brian. B-R-I-A-N.

Girl: What's your address?

Brian: It's 55 Isabel Street, Coral Gables.

Andy: The ZIP code is 33134.

Girl: And what's your phone number?

Brian: Let me see . . . It's (305) 555-1366.

Girl: Excuse me. Can you repeat that, please?

Brian: Sure . . . (305) 555-1366.

Girl: What's your date of birth, Brian?

Brian: October 15th, 1988.

Girl: OK. Here's your pass. Is there anything else?

Brian: No, that's it. Thanks!

2 Comprehension

Work with a partner. Fill out Brian's guest pass.

GUEST PASS

Valid for September 21 only

Last name: _____

First name: _____

Date of birth: _____

Address: _____

_____

Phone number: _____

Signature: _____

3 Your Turn

Fill out the membership form with your information. If an item does not apply to you, leave it blank.

Membership Application Form

/ /

Last name | First name | Date of birth

Address

State

Home phone | E-mail

Signature

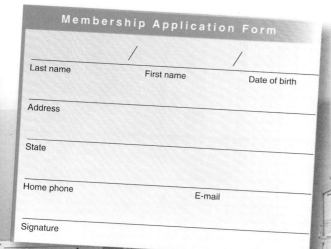

4 Communication

Giving your name and address

Make a directory in your notebook. Ask for the names, addresses, and telephone numbers of five classmates. Use the questions below.

What's your name?
Can you spell your last name?
What's your address?
What's your telephone number?
Can you repeat that, please?

Name	Address	Telephone number

5 Vocabulary

Months of the year

A. Work with a partner. Unscramble the letters to form the names of the months.

1. J _ _ _ _ _ _   7. J _ _ _
   rjnyaua   yjlu
2. F _ _ _ _ _ _ _   8. A _ _ _ _ _
   ybufraer   utagsu
3. M _ _ _ _   9. S _ _ _ _ _ _ _ _
   hmrac   bestmrpee
4. A _ _ _ _   10. O _ _ _ _ _ _
   ralpi   broocet
5. M _ _   11. N _ _ _ _ _ _ _
   yam   vbenreom
6. J _ _ _   12. D _ _ _ _ _ _ _
   nuej   becderem

B. 🎧 Now listen and repeat.

PILATES

YMCA
IS NOT RESPONSIBLE
FOR VALUABLES

PLEASE UTILIZE OUR
LOCKERS

6 Dialogue

Don't listen to the audio yet. Read the dialogue quickly. Then do Exercise 7.

Brian: Hey, Andy, check this out.
They have a new volleyball league.

Andy: Cool. When's the first game?

Brian: It's next month, on October 5th. And look at this. "Peewee baseball league." What's a "Peewee league?"

Andy: Oh, it's baseball for little kids.

Brian: That sounds fun. When's the signup?

Andy: It's next Saturday the 28th. Wait a minute. What's today's date?

Brian: It's the 21st.

Andy: Oh no! I'm dead!

Brian: Why? What's the problem?

Andy: Yesterday was Caroline's birthday!

Brian: Who's Caroline?

Andy: She's my girlfriend. Oh, man!

Brian: Yeah, man. You're in big trouble.

7 Comprehension

🎧 **Scan the dialogue and fill in the missing information. Now, read the dialogue carefully and check your answers. Then listen.**

_____ 1. The date of the volleyball game

_____ 2. What a Peewee baseball league is

_____ 3. The name of Andy's girlfriend

_____ 4. The date of her birthday

8 Vocabulary

Ordinal numbers: 1st–10th

A. 🎧 **Listen and repeat.**

1st	2nd	3rd	4th	5th
first	second	third	fourth	fifth

6th	7th	8th	9th	10th
sixth	seventh	eighth	ninth	tenth

B. Now work with a partner. Say three cardinal numbers at random. Your partner says the corresponding ordinal numbers.

A: Three, nine, one   B: Third, ninth, first

9 Practice

Have a competition! Go to page 89.

GRAMMAR FOCUS

Information questions with *be*; Prepositions of time: *in, on*

Question word	be		Answer
Who	**is**	your English teacher?	Ms. Moser.
What	**is**	today's date?	It's June 13th.
What day	**is**	it?	It's Monday.
How old	**are**	you?	I'm 12 years old.
Where	**are**	your books?	They're under my desk.
When	**is**	your birthday?	It's in January. *OR* It's on January 11th.

Remember! Use *in* with months and *on* with exact dates.
Who is = **Who's**   What is = **What's**

10 Practice

Look at the underlined parts of the answers.
Write a question for each answer.

1. The English test is on <u>Friday</u>.
   When is the English test?

2. Brian is <u>15 years old</u>.

_____

3. Annie is <u>Liza's best friend</u>.

_____

4. Brian's parents are in <u>Australia</u>.

_____

5. Today's date is <u>February 12th</u>.

_____

11 Practice

Have a competition! Go to page 89.

12 Vocabulary

Ordinal numbers: 11th –21st

🎧 **Listen and repeat.**

11th	eleventh	**16th**	sixteenth
12th	twelfth	**17th**	seventeenth
13th	thirteenth	**18th**	eighteenth
14th	fourteenth	**19th**	nineteenth
15th	fifteenth	**20th**	twentieth

But look! **21st** ➝ twenty-first

13 Communication

Giving the date of your birthday

A. 🎧 Listen and read.

A: When's your birthday?
B: It's on August 28th.

B. Take a survey of birthdays in your class. In your notebook, make a chart like the one below.

C. Check your chart of birthdays every month. Invite the class to sing "Happy Birthday" to students who have birthdays that month.

MONTH	CLASSMATES' NAMES
January	Kristina (12th)
February	
March	
April	
May	

14 Reading

Look at the ad. Scan the ad and answer the questions below.

1. In what months are the night classes at Palm High School?
   In March, April, and May.

2. When is the chess class?
   _____

3. Where is the guitar class?
   _____

4. What classes are on Wednesday?
   _____

5. What is the phone number to call?
   _____

15 Listening

A. ∩ Listen and fill in the form.

Palm High School Night Classes

Last name: _Akiyama_   First name: _____

Tel. no.: _____   Date of birth: _____

Are you a student at Palm H.S.?

Yes _____   No _____

Course: _____   Day: _____

B. Exchange work with a classmate. Correct each other's mistakes.

16 Speaking

Work with a partner. Ask each other questions about the ad and about the information in Annie's form.

A. What's Annie's phone number?
B. It's 555-1244.

Learn to Learn

Asking for help and clarification

Ask for help when you need it. It shows that you are an interested learner. Here are some useful expressions to use:

- Can you repeat that, please?
- Can you explain that again, please?
- Can you spell that, please?
- Can you speak more slowly, please?

Progress Check *Units 3 and 4*

Grammar

A. Fill in the chart. (2 points each)

Singular	Plural	Plural	Singular
car	*cars*	addresses	
boy		men	
city		classes	
nationality		children	
language		people	

B. Change the sentences to plural. (3 points each)

1. That fax is for you.
   Those faxes are for you.

2. This dictionary is good.
   _____

3. That man is from Chile.
   _____

4. That woman is nice.
   _____

C. Fill in the blanks with *a* or *an*. (1 point each)

1. Brian is __*an*__ exchange student.
2. Mel Gibson is _____ actor.
3. Eric is _____ student.
4. Japanese is _____ difficult language.
5. A Fiat is _____ Italian car.

D. Write the questions for the answers below. (2 points each)

1. *Where are you from?*
   I'm from New York.
2. _____
   The capital of Brazil is Brasilia.
3. _____
   They are Canadian.
4. _____
   He's 25 years old.

E. Fill in the blanks with *in* or *on*. (1 point each)

1. My birthday is __*in*__ August.
2. The party is _____ Sunday.
3. Our meeting is _____ Friday.
4. In Canada, winter starts _____ December.
5. Halloween is _____ October 31st.

Vocabulary

F. Rewrite the sentences. State each person's nationality. (3 points each)

1. Sophia Loren is from Italy.
   She is Italian.

2. That man is from Korea.
   _____

3. Those students are from Spain.
   _____

4. These children are from China.
   _____

G. Unscramble the letters to find the months. Then write sentences. (2 points each)

1. iparl   *April is the fourth month.*
2. beeemprst _____
3. uugats   _____
4. rebcoot _____
5. hcamr   _____

Communication

H. Work with a partner. Ask each other these questions. (3 points each)

1. What's your name?
2. Can you spell your name, please?
3. What's your address?
4. What's your phone number?
5. When's your birthday?

SONG

Vanessa Amorosi

Vanessa Amorosi, a star in her home country of Australia, started dancing and singing when she was 4 years old. At 15, she was discovered while performing at a Russian restaurant. She performed the song "Absolutely Everybody" at the closing ceremony of the Sydney 2000 Olympic Games.

Absolutely Everybody

Absolutely everybody,
Everybody needs a little loving,
Everybody needs somebody thinking of them.
Everybody needs a little respect,
And whatever it takes, I'm gonna get it.

Everybody needs a hand to hold,
Someone to cling to when the nights
are getting cold.
I'm no different, I am just the same,
A player in the game.

Chorus

Absolutely everybody, everybody, everybody.
Absolutely everybody in the whole wide world.
Everybody breathes, and everybody needs.
Absolutely Everybody

Everybody needs a human touch.
I can't live without it, it means too much to me.
Everybody needs one true friend,
Someone who'll be there 'til the very end.

And absolutely everybody breathes,
And everybody, everybody bleeds.
We're no different, we're all the same,
A player in the game.

Repeat Chorus

Absolutely everybody.
Every boy and girl, every woman and child.
Every father and son, I said now everyone,
Yes now everyone.

Everybody needs a human touch.
Everybody, everybody needs love.
I'm no different, I am just the same,
A player in the game.

Repeat Chorus

1. ⌒ Read and listen to the song. Then read the lyrics again and circle all the verbs in the simple present tense.

2. Work with a partner. List the things people need according to the song. Compare your list with a partner's list.

3. Discuss as a class: What message did you get from this song?

GAME *Heads or Tails*

1. Get a coin and game piece for yourself.
2. Flip the coin to decide who goes first.
3. Begin at "Start" and flip the coin. For heads, move one space, and ask a question based on the picture. For tails move two spaces and make a sentence based on the picture. If you make a mistake, move back one space.
4. Take turns. The first person to cross the finish line wins.

What?	Who?
When?	Is?
Where?	Are?

5 I have two sisters.

Learning Goals

Communication
Talk about your family
Ask what people look like

Grammar
Possessive nouns
Simple present tense: *have*
Any in questions and negatives

Vocabulary
Family members
Physical description

1 Vocabulary

Family members

A. ⌂ **Look at Andy's family tree as you listen.
Listen again and repeat.**

Andy Gibson's Family

grandmother
Martha

grandfather
Bruno

mother
Gloria

father
Joe

aunt
Connie

uncle
Steve

Andy

sister
Liza

brother
Robbie

cousin
Joey

2 Practice

Work with a partner. Can you guess the family terms? Write them in the blanks. You may use a dictionary.

1. grandfather and grandmother =
   grandparents

2. father and mother = _____

3. son and daughter = _____

4. grandson and granddaughter =
   _____

GRAMMAR FOCUS

Possessive nouns

Singular nouns: add 's
Andy is Liza**'s** brother.
This is my son**'s** picture.

Most plural nouns: add ' (apostrophe)
Liza is the boy**s'** sister.
These are my daughter**s'** pictures.

(Remember!) Add **'s** to irregular plural nouns to form the possessive.

Examples of irregular nouns
women**'s** jeans   children**'s** school
men**'s** jeans   people**'s** meeting

3 Practice

Add **'s** or **'** to the nouns in parentheses.

1. _____Andy's_____ last name is Gibson. (Andy)

2. His _____ names are Joe and Gloria. (parents)

3. Joey is _____ cousin. (Liza)

4. The _____ names are Robbie and Andy. (brothers)

5. Their _____ name is Connie. (aunt)

6. Connie is _____ mother. (Joey)

4 Practice

Have a competition! Go to page 90.

5 Communication

Talking about your family

On a piece of paper, draw your family tree. Label your family tree *mother, father,* etc., but do not write the people's names. Exchange family trees with a classmate. Fill in the names of the people in your partner's family.

A: What are your grandparents' names?
B: Oscar and Alicia.

6 Dialogue

🎧 **Read quickly. Who is Robbie's cousin? Then listen and read again.**

Dad: So, Brian, do you have any brothers or sisters?

Brian: I have two sisters, but I don't have any brothers.

Andy: What do they look like? Do you have any pictures of them?

Brian: Yes, I do. Here they are. The blond one is Sandy, and the one with brown hair is Louise.

Mom: They're very pretty. How about cousins? How many cousins do you have?

Brian: I have 12 cousins.

Robbie: That's a lot of cousins. We have only one cousin.

Joey: And that's me!

Robbie: *(Whispering)* Brian, do you have a girlfriend?

Brian: No, I don't, Robbie.

Robbie: Andy has a girlfriend. Her name's Caroline. Liza doesn't have a . . .

Liza: Robbie!

7 Comprehension

Read the sentences. Cross out the wrong information. Then correct the sentences.

1. Brian has ~~three~~ *two* sisters.
2. His sisters' names are Louise and Carla.
3. Sandy has black hair.
4. Liza and Joey are sisters.
5. Andy's girlfriend is Sandy.

GRAMMAR FOCUS

Simple present tense: *have*

Affirmative statements			Negative statements		
He/She	**has**	a sister.	He/She	**doesn't have**	any sisters.
It	**has**	four bedrooms.	It	**doesn't have**	four bedrooms.
I/You/We/They	**have**	two sisters.	I/You/We/They	**don't have**	any sisters.

Remember! Use *any* in negative statements.

Yes/No questions			Affirmative answers			Negative answers		
Does	it	**have** *any* bedrooms?	Yes,	it	**does**.	No,	it	**doesn't**.
Does	he/she	**have** *any* sisters?	Yes,	he/she	**does**.	No,	he/she	**doesn't**.
Do	you/I/we/they	**have** *any* sisters?	Yes,	I/you/we/they	**do**.	No,	I/you/we/they	**don't**.

Remember! Use *any* in *Yes/No* questions.

8 Practice

A. Fill in the blanks with *has* and *have*.

My name's Jeff. I ___*have*___ a big, happy family. I (1) _____ twin sisters and two brothers. My grandmother lives with us.

My parents (2) _____ a nice house. It's big. It (3) _____ four bedrooms. I am the big brother, so I (4) _____ a room just for me!

What do my twin sisters look like? Well, they (5) _____ blond hair and blue eyes, just like my grandmother's. My brothers and I (6) _____ brown hair and brown eyes. My parents (7) _____ brown eyes. But my father (8) _____ brown hair, and my mother (9) _____ blond hair.

B. Copy the sentences in your notebook. Change the negative statements to affirmative statements.

1. Jeff doesn't have a happy family.
   Jeff has a happy family.
2. Jeff doesn't have any brothers and sisters.
3. Jeff's parents don't have a big house.
4. The twin sisters don't have blond hair.
5. Jeff's mother doesn't have brown eyes.

9 Practice

Unscramble the words to make *Yes/No* questions. Then work with a partner. Ask each other the questions. Answer using your own information.

1. have/cousins/Do/any/you
   Do you have any cousins?
2. your father/have/Does/brothers/any
   _____?
3. Do/any/have/you/aunts
   _____?
4. your best friend/have/any/Does/sisters
   _____?

10 Vocabulary

Physical description

A. Look at the photos and the words in the boxes. Draw a line from the color adjective to the person that has that color eyes or hair. Use each description only once.

Sarah Ferguson

Keanu Reeves

Brad Pitt

Charlize Theron

| Eye color | gray | blue | green | brown |

| Hair color | brown | red | blond | black |

B. Work with a partner. Ask and answer questions about the people in the pictures.

A: What does Brad Pitt look like?
B: He has brown hair and gray eyes.

11 Your Turn

A. Work in groups of three. Do a survey on families. Copy the chart in your notebook. Ask these questions:

Do you have a big family?
Who are the members of your family?
How many sisters do you have?
How many brothers do you have?

Name	Family members	Total	No. of sisters	No. of brothers
Maria	Tomas, Ana, James, Maria	4	0	1

B. Ask each other questions about what the members of your families look like.

12 Pronunciation

Rising and falling intonation in questions

A. 🎧 Listen and repeat.

1. Do you have any sisters?
2. What's your cousin's name?
3. What do they look like?
4. Does she have blue eyes?
5. Does he have a big family?

B. 🎧 Listen. Do the questions have a rising or falling intonation? Circle your answer.

1. rising   falling
2. rising   falling
3. rising   falling
4. rising   falling

At Caroline's

A. Before you listen, write the missing lines in the dialogue.
Choose from the box.

B. 🎧 Listen and check your answers.

> What does he look like?
> But I have time now.
> Can I meet this Brian?
> An Australian with blue eyes.

1
Oh, it's you.
I'm sorry I missed your birthday. I'm very busy.

2
And why are you busy?
You know.
Oh, yeah. It's Brian again.
Yes, it's Brian. He's new here, so we have a lot to do. (1) _____

3
Gee, thanks. Brian first, me second.
Caroline, please. Try to understand.

4
(2) _____
Sure.
Hey, what about me? I'm your boyfriend, remember?

5
(3) _____
Well, he has blue eyes and blond hair. He's from Australia.

6
Ooh.
(4) _____
I like that.
I know, but you don't have time for me, remember?

6 Do you like hip-hop music?

Learning Goals

Communication
Talk about likes and dislikes
Describe people

Grammar
Simple present tense: *like*
  Statements
  Yes/No questions
Adjectives: *be* + adjective
           adjective + noun

Vocabulary
More physical description

1 Dialogue

🎧 **Listen and read. Circle the different types of music in the dialogue.**

Brian: Oh, wow! This place is awesome!

Andy: Yeah, I know. So, what kind of music do you like, Brian?

Brian: Well, I like different kinds. My favorite is rock. I don't like hip-hop.

Andy: I love hip-hop. I like rap, too. Do you like heavy metal?

Brian: Oh, no. I hate it. How about Liza? Does she like hip-hop and heavy metal?

Andy: No. She likes pop music. And Robbie likes anything loud and noisy.

Brian: Robbie's a cool kid. What do your parents like?

Andy: My mom loves Celine Dion. My dad doesn't. He likes Faith Hill.

Brian: You have cool parents. My dad likes Pavarotti. You should hear him sing like Pavarotti. It's awful!

2 Comprehension

Write the kind of music or the singer each person likes and does not like.

	Likes	Does not like
1. Brian	rock	hip-hop, heavy metal
2. Andy		
3. Liza		

GRAMMAR FOCUS

Simple present tense: *like*

Affirmative statements		Negative statements	
I You We They	**like** hip-hop music.	I You We They	**don't like** hip-hop music.
He She	**likes** hip-hop music.	He She	**doesn't like** hip-hop music.

3 Practice

Read the dialogue again. Fill in the blanks with *like, likes, don't like,* or *doesn't like.*

1. They _____*like*_____ music.

2. Brian _____ rock music.

3. He _____ hip-hop.

4. Andy _____ hip-hop.

5. Brian and Liza _____ heavy metal.

6. Robbie _____ loud music.

4 Your Turn

In your notebook, write sentences about what each person in your family likes or does not like. Read your sentences to the class.

5 Pronunciation

The sounds /ɑ/ and /ɔ/

A. ⌒ Listen and repeat.

/ɑ/	/ɔ/
hot	hall
Tom	tall
Don	Dawn

B. ⌒ Listen. Circle the words with the /ɑ/ sound.

1. Is it Don or Dawn?
2. It's hot in the hall.
3. This is awesome!

GRAMMAR FOCUS

Simple present tense: *like*

Yes/No questions with *do*

Do	I you we they	**like** music?
Does	he she	**like** music?

Affirmative answers

Yes,	I you we they	**do**.
Yes,	he she	**does**.

Negative answers

No,	I you we they	**don't**.
No,	he she	**doesn't**.

1. Gloria Estefan   2. JC Chasez

3. Mandy Moore

6 Practice

Read the answers. Write *Yes/No* **questions.**

1. *Do you like English?*

   Yes, I do. I like English.

2. _____

   No, she doesn't. My mother doesn't like ballet.

3. _____

   Yes, they do. Our teachers like classical music.

4. _____

   Yes, they do. My friends like sports.

5. _____

   No, he doesn't. My father doesn't like scary movies.

7 Communication

Talking about likes and dislikes

A. Work with a partner. Ask your partner if he or she likes the following:

music	computers	video games
ballet	sports	school

A: Do you like music?
B: Yes, I do.

B. Join another pair. Tell them what your partner likes and doesn't like.

A: Mike likes music. He doesn't like ballet.

5. Lance Bass

4. Jennifer Lopez

6. Pavarotti

GRAMMAR FOCUS

Be + adjective	Adjective + noun
She's **tall**.	She's a **tall** girl. OR The **tall** girl is my sister.
His hair is **long**.	He has **long** hair.

3. Mandy Moore (*thin*): _____

4. Jennifer Lopez (*long hair*): _____

5. Lance Bass (*short hair*): _____

6. Pavarotti (*heavy*): _____

8 Vocabulary

More physical description

A. 🎧 Listen and repeat as you look at the pictures.

Height	Body size	Hair length	Hair style
tall	heavy	long	straight
medium height	medium build	medium length	wavy
short	thin	short	curly

B. Look at the pictures. Write sentences about them, using the adjectives and the names below.

1. Gloria Estefan (*short*): *Gloria Estefan is short.*

2. JC Chasez (*tall*): _____

9 Listening

A. 🎧 Listen and draw each person in your notebook. Label your drawings. Then color the hair and eyes.

B. 🎧 Exchange drawings with a partner. Listen again and check your work.

10 Speaking

Work with a partner. Think of a classmate. Describe this person to your partner. Your partner will guess who it is.

A: She's thin. She has short hair and brown eyes. She likes pop music.

B: Is she Paula?

A: No. Guess again. Her hair is wavy.

11 Reading

Read the article on Wade Robson.

Wade Robson, King of the Dance

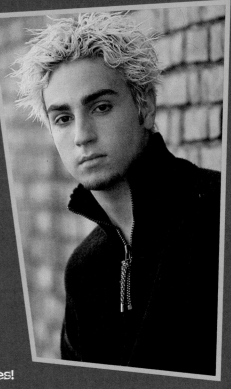

Wade is a teenager, just like you. But superstars Britney Spears and the members of the 'NSync band love him. These superstars do what Wade tells them to do. Why? Wade Robson is their teacher!

Wade started dancing at the age of two. As a child, he loved watching Michael Jackson's Thriller. He liked those cool dance steps, especially the Moon Walk. At age five, Wade was already a dance champion.

Wade is originally from Australia. Now he lives with his family in Los Angeles, California. The family was poor. But Hollywood noticed Wade's awesome dance talent. Wade is now rich and calls Britney Spears and the members of 'NSync his friends! When you see Britney Spears' famous 2001 Pepsi commercial, think of Wade. Those are his moves!

12 Writing

A. Answer the questions below. Use complete sentences.

1. Who is Wade Robson?

   _____

2. Where is he from?

   _____

3. Who is his idol?

   _____

4. Who are his famous students?

   _____

B. In your notebook, list five words and expressions from the reading that you want to learn. Look them up in a dictionary. Use them in sentences.

Progress Check *Units 5 and 6*

Grammar

A. Look at the chart. Then complete the sentences with *has, have, doesn't have,* or *don't have.* (2 points each)

	Car	Sister	Uncle	Son	Daughter
Peter	√			√	√
Mario	√	√			
Vivien	√	√			

1. I'm Peter. I _____don't have_____ a sister.
2. Mario _____ a daughter.
3. We _____ any uncles.
4. Vivien _____ a sister.
5. We all _____ a car.
6. Mario and Vivien _____ any children.

B. Complete the questions with the verbs in parentheses. Then answer the questions, using short answers and contractions when possible. (2 points each)

1. __Do__ you __have__ a family in Japan? *(have)*
   No, _I_ __don't.__
2. _____ she _____ cats? *(like)*
   Yes, _____.
3. _____ they _____ a computer? *(have)*
   No, _____.
4. _____ Anne _____ any children? *(have)*
   Yes, _____.
5. _____ your parents _____ music? *(like)*
   Yes, _____.
6. _____ he _____ hip-hop? *(like)*
   No, _____.
7. _____ Kim _____ a pet? *(have)*
   Yes, _____.

C. Circle the correct word to complete each sentence. (1 point each)

1. Her (*brothers'*/*brother's*) rooms are messy.
2. Britney is (*Justin's*/*Justins'*) girlfriend.
3. My (*parents'*/*parent's*) car is new.
4. His (*sister's*/*sisters'*) names are Ann and Tina.

Vocabulary

D. Write each word in the correct column. (1 point each)

blue	reggae	tall
brown	heavy	pop
thin	classical	gray

Music	Colors	Physical description
reggae		

E. Match the phrases with the words. (1 point each)

1. my mother's father	aunt
2. my father's sister	cousins
3. my uncle's children	parents
4. my parents' daughter	uncle
5. our mother and father	grandfather
6. my mother's brother	sister

Communication

F. Work with a partner. Ask each other these questions. (3 points each)

1. How many brothers do you have?
2. Do you have any sisters?
3. What color are your eyes?
4. What kind of music do you like?
5. What's your teacher's name?

1 Reading

A. Scan the article on the right for difficult words. List them in your notebook and look up their meanings in the dictionary. Then read the article.

B. Circle the correct answer to complete the sentences.

1. A *survey* is a ____.
   - a. study
   - b. TV show
   - c. magazine

2. When you're *affectionate,* you show ____.
   - a. love
   - b. sadness
   - c. anger

3. A family that *gets along* has people who ____.
   - a. always fight
   - b. are happy together
   - c. don't talk to each other

4. A *hero* is someone you ____.
   - a. respect a lot
   - b. don't care about
   - c. dislike

2 Speaking

Do this as homework: Interview an older person in your family. Ask these questions.

1. What's your opinion of teenagers today?
2. What do you like about teenagers?
3. What don't you like about teenagers?

3 Writing

A. Write the results of your interview in English. If you need help, work with a friend or family member who speaks English.

B. Share the results of your interview with the class.

"The Kids Are Alright"

In TV shows and movies, teenagers are often angry and unhappy. But according to a recent survey, most of today's young people are affectionate, reasonable, and happy. In other words, teenagers are not so bad after all.

The survey says that most teenagers get along well with their parents. Though teens go to their friends for advice on music and clothes, they go to their parents when they have a problem. They ask their parents for advice on college and careers. Most teenagers think that their parents understand and love them. Many even think that their parents are cool!

Of course, teenagers keep secrets from their parents, but these are usually just teen items such as diaries, CDs, and magazines.

And who do teenagers choose for their heroes? Many teens choose a family member, not a singer or an actor. Most teens say they like spending time with both parents and friends.

In short, today's teenagers are very nice kids. As the band The Who used to sing, the kids are all right.

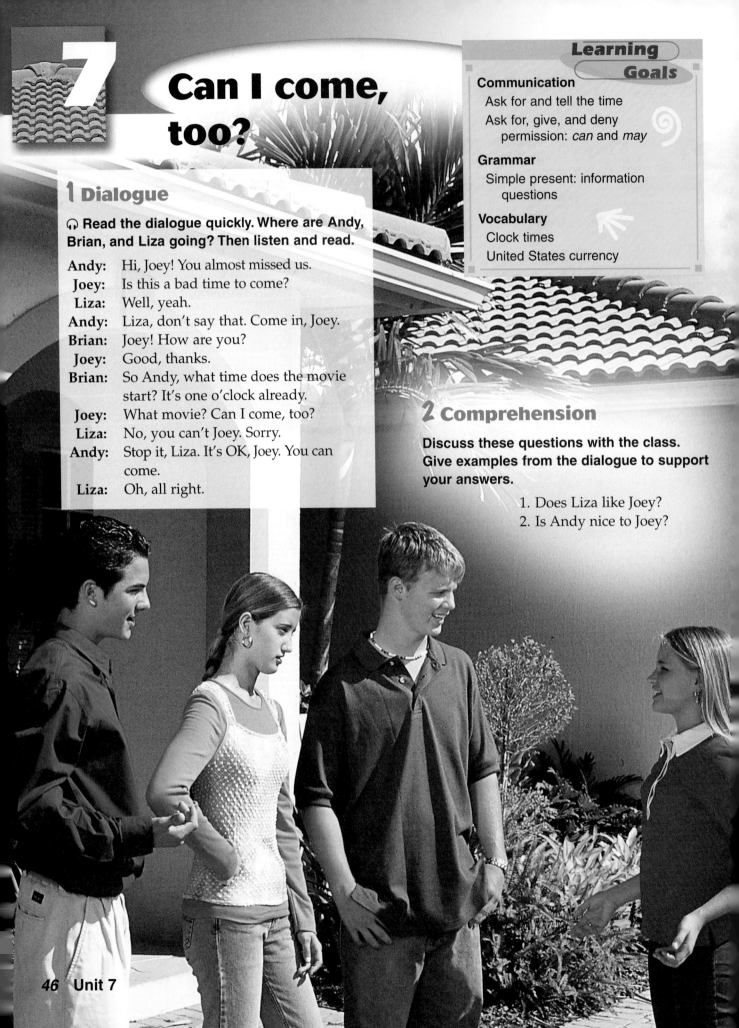

7 Can I come, too?

Learning Goals

Communication
Ask for and tell the time
Ask for, give, and deny permission: *can* and *may*

Grammar
Simple present: information questions

Vocabulary
Clock times
United States currency

1 Dialogue

🎧 **Read the dialogue quickly. Where are Andy, Brian, and Liza going? Then listen and read.**

Andy: Hi, Joey! You almost missed us.
Joey: Is this a bad time to come?
Liza: Well, yeah.
Andy: Liza, don't say that. Come in, Joey.
Brian: Joey! How are you?
Joey: Good, thanks.
Brian: So Andy, what time does the movie start? It's one o'clock already.
Joey: What movie? Can I come, too?
Liza: No, you can't Joey. Sorry.
Andy: Stop it, Liza. It's OK, Joey. You can come.
Liza: Oh, all right.

2 Comprehension

Discuss these questions with the class. Give examples from the dialogue to support your answers.

1. Does Liza like Joey?
2. Is Andy nice to Joey?

3 Useful Phrases

A. 🎧 **Listen and repeat.**

- You almost missed us.
- Is this a bad time?
- Hurry up.
- Stop it.

B. What expressions from Exercise A are appropriate to say for these situations?

1. You and your sister are running late.
2. You are visiting your best friend. She looks busy.

4 Vocabulary

Clock times

A. 🎧 **Look at the clock above. Listen and repeat.**

B. Ask a partner about the time. Write the time next to each clock.

A: What time is it?   B: It's a quarter after eleven.

after
o'clock
five to / five after
ten to / ten after
a quarter to / a quarter after
twenty to / twenty after
twenty-five to / twenty-five after
thirty
to

GRAMMAR FOCUS

Simple present tense: information questions

Questions	Answers
Who **does** Liza **like**?	She likes Brian.
Why **does** Liza **like** Brian?	Because he's nice and he's cute.
What **do** they **do** on Saturdays?	They hang out at a friend's house.
When **does** Joey **visit** her cousins?	She visits them after school.
What time **does** the movie **start**?	It starts at 1 P.M.

Remember! Use the preposition *at* with a specific time.

5 Practice

Make questions. Write them in your notebook.

1. live/does/Where/Andy/?

   Where does Andy live?

2. Liza/like/Why/Joey/doesn't/?
3. start/What time/your English class/does/?
4. the students/When/the computers/do/use/?
5. do/like/What colors/you?

6 Information Gap

Student A, go to page 91. Student B, go to page 92. Follow the instructions.

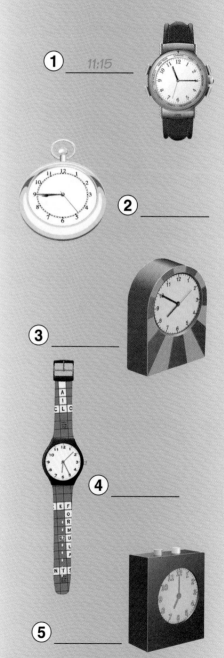

① _____ 11:15

② _____

③ _____

④ _____

⑤ _____

7 Dialogue

🎧 **Listen and read. How much is an adult ticket?**

Joey: I'll get the tickets, Andy.

Andy: OK. Here's our money.

Robbie: Can I go with you, Joey? Please?

Joey: Sure. C'mon. OK. Tell the lady what you want, Robbie.

Robbie: Hello. Five tickets, please. Four adult tickets and one child.

Clerk: What movie?

Robbie: The dinosaur one, at 2:30.

Clerk: OK. That's four adult tickets and one child ticket.

Robbie: Right. How much are the tickets?

Clerk: $28.50. The child's ticket is $4.50.

Joey: Here's the money, Robbie.

Robbie: OK. Here you are.

Clerk: Thank you. Here are your tickets. Enjoy the movie.

8 Comprehension

Write the answers in the blanks.

1. What time does the movie start?

   _____

2. What movie does the group want to see?

   _____

3. How much do the tickets cost all together?

   _____

4. How much does Robbie's ticket cost?

   _____

9 Vocabulary

United States currency

🎧 **Look at the pictures. Listen and repeat.**

1. a penny = one cent = 1¢

2. a nickel = five cents = 5¢

3. a dime = ten cents = 10¢

4. a quarter = twenty-five cents = 25¢

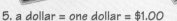
5. a dollar = one dollar = $1.00

6. five dollars = $5.00

7. ten dollars = $10.00

8. twenty dollars = $20.00

10 Practice

Write the amounts in numbers.

1. a dollar = _$1.00_
2. a quarter = _____
3. twenty dollars = _____
4. a dime = _____
5. a penny = _____
6. a nickel = _____

11 Listening

A. 🎧 **Listen and circle the amount you hear.**

1. a. $10.00   b. 10¢
2. a. 25¢   b. $25.00
3. a. $1.00   b. 10¢
4. a. $1.00   b. 1¢
5. a. 50¢   b. $5.00
6. a. 75¢   b. $75.00

B. 🎧 **Listen again and check your work.**

12 Practice

Work with a partner. Take turns asking and answering money questions like the example below.

A: How much are three dimes?
B: Thirty cents.

13 Communication

Asking for permission

A. 🎧 **Listen and read.**

Robbie: Can I come in, Liza?

Liza: No, you can't. Say *may* and ask me again.

Robbie: *May* I come in, please?

Liza: Yes, you may. Please come in, Robbie.

Robbie: Thank you.

Remember, you can use *may* or *can* to ask for permission. But *may* is more polite and more formal than *can*.

B. Work with a partner. In your notebook, write two dialogues for one of the following situations. Dialogue 1 gives permission; Dialogue 2 refuses permission.

1. You are in your brother's room. Ask permission to use his CD player.
2. Your parents' room is closed. You need to talk to your mom. Ask permission to come in.
3. You want to borrow your friend's magazine. Ask permission.
4. You need to go out during class. Ask permission from your teacher.

Dialogue 1
A: Can I use your CD player?
B: Sure.

Dialogue 2
A: Can I use your CD player?
B: No, you can't. Sorry.

14 Pronunciation

The sounds /æ/ and /ɑ/

A. 🎧 **Listen and repeat.**

/æ/	/ɑ/
can	car
can't	cart
map	Mark

B. 🎧 **Listen. Circle the words with the /æ/ sound.**

1. There's a packet of sugar in my pocket.
2. I can't read this odd ad.
3. Mark uses a map when he drives.

At the Amusement Park

🎧 **Listen and read the dialogue. Who doesn't have any money?**

8 I always get up at 6:30.

Learning Goals

Communication
Talk about daily routines

Grammar
Sequence words: *first, then, after that*

Simple present with adverbs of frequency: *always, usually, often, sometimes, never*

Vocabulary
Daily routines

1 Reading

Read about Brian's daily routine. What day is his favorite?

My Life in Australia

Every morning my alarm goes off at 6:30. No problem. I usually hit the snooze button and close my eyes again. But I can never go back to sleep, so I get up.

I do the same things every day. First, I take a shower. Then, I brush my teeth and get dressed. After that, I have breakfast. On weekdays, breakfast is always quick. I sometimes have cereal, but I usually just grab a banana. Then I run to the bus stop.

School starts at 8:30 A.M. I'm never late for school. I'm always in my class just before the bell rings. Call it great timing. I call it a mad rush!

Lunch is at 12:30 and school ends at 3:00. But I never get home until after 6:00 P.M. I am on the track-and-field team, and I practice after school. After practice, I usually go to the gym. On Saturdays, my team often competes with teams from other schools. I am always tired after every competition, but I don't mind. I love running.

Sunday is my favorite day. It's usually my lazy day, and I love it!

2 Comprehension

A. Answer these questions orally.

1. What does Brian usually do after school?
2. What does Brian do on Saturdays?
3. What sport does Brian play?

B. Match the sentences with the pictures.

___4___ a. Brian has lunch at school.

_____ b. He takes the bus.

_____ c. He gets up at 6:30.

_____ d. He starts school at 8:30 A.M.

_____ e. After school, he has track practice.

3 Pronunciation

The sounds /s/, /z/, /ɪz/

A. ∩ Listen and repeat.

/s/	/z/	/ɪz/
eats	does	catches
walks	ends	practices

B. ∩ Listen. Circle the verbs. In each blank, write the ending sound (/s/, /z/, or /ɪz/) of the verbs.

_____ 1. Brian wakes up at 6:30. He takes the bus to school.

_____ 2. He brushes his teeth. Then he watches TV.

_____ 3. He leaves home at 7:30. He goes to school by bus.

4 Vocabulary

Daily routines

A. 🎧 Listen and repeat.

B. Number the activities 1–9 according to your routine on school days.

___3___ brush my teeth

_____ do homework

_____ have breakfast

_____ go to school

_____ get up

_____ eat dinner

_____ take a shower

_____ get home from school

GRAMMAR FOCUS

Sequence words: *first, then, after that*

First, the alarm rings.
Then, I hit the snooze button.
After that, I get up.

_____ watch TV

5 Practice

A. Read page 52 again. Circle the sequence words.

B. Write three things that Brian does on a school day. Use *first, then,* and *after that.*

1. _____

2. _____

3. _____

6 Communication

Talking about daily routines

Work with a partner. Talk about your activities on Sundays.

A: What do you do on Sundays?
B: Well, I stay in bed all morning. When I get up, I check my e-mail. Then, I take a shower. After that, I have breakfast. How about you?

54 Unit 8

GRAMMAR FOCUS

Adverbs of frequency

	0%	100%
always	██████████████████	
usually	███████████████	
often	███████████	
sometimes	██████	
never		

I **always** have breakfast in the morning.
I **usually** do my homework in the evening.
I **often** have cereal for breakfast.
I **sometimes** sleep on the bus.
I **never** go to school on Sundays.

Remember! Adverbs of frequency come *before* the main verb, but *after* the verb *be*.

I am **always** busy.

7 Practice

A. Work with a partner. Take turns asking each other the questions in the questionnaire below. Record your partner's answers by putting a check (√) in the appropriate place.

A: What do you have for breakfast?
B: I always have cereal and milk. I sometimes have bread and butter. I never have coffee.

B. Share the completed questionnaire with another pair.

Your Daily Routine

	Always	Usually	Often	Sometimes	Never
What do you have for breakfast?					
• coffee					✔
• juice					
• cereal with milk	✔				
• bread and butter				✔	
How do you go to school?					
• by car					
• by bus					
• walk					
What do you do after school?					
• see friends					
• participate in after-school activities					
• go home					
What do you do in the evening?					
• use the computer					
• do homework					
• watch TV with my family					
• listen to music					

8 Reading

A. Study the graph of a teenager's typical weekday.

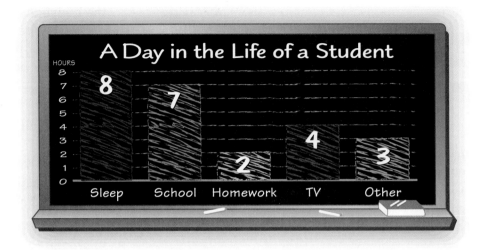

A Day in the Life of a Student

HOURS: 8, 7, 6, 5, 4, 3, 2, 1, 0

Sleep 8 · School 7 · Homework 2 · TV 4 · Other 3

B. As a class, answer the questions orally.

1. Does the student get eight hours of sleep?
2. How many hours per day does the student spend on homework?
3. How many hours per day does the student spend watching TV?
4. Have a class discussion. Is four hours a day in front of the TV a good use of time? Why or why not?

9 Listening

🎧 Listen to Julie describe her typical day. Listen again and complete the chart.

Activity	Time
Gets up	6 A.M.
Bus picks her up	
School starts	
School ends	
Gets home	
Has dinner	
Goes to bed	

10 Writing

In your notebook, write about your typical day. Compare your typical day with Brian's and Julie's. Whose day is similar to yours?

11 Your Turn

A. Work in groups of three. List the names of students in your group. Find out how many hours a day each student spends on daily activities.

A: How many hours do you sleep each day?
B: I usually sleep eight hours.

B. Post the results on the class bulletin board.

Activities	Michael		
Sleeps	8 hours		
Does homework	2 hours		
Watches TV	2 hours		
Uses the computer	45 minutes		
Reads	1 hour		

Progress Check *Units 7 and 8*

Grammar

A. Complete the sentences with *in*, *on*, or *at*. (2 points each)

1. My birthday is ___in___ January.
2. The competition is _____ Friday.
3. My English class starts _____ 7:45 A.M.
4. In Brazil, summer starts _____ December.
5. We go to bed _____ 10 P.M.

B. Fill in the blanks with *is*, *are*, *do*, or *does*. (2 points each)

1. What time __does__ the movie start?
2. When _____ our volleyball practice?
3. Where _____ your books?
4. What _____ your sister study in college?
5. What time _____ the stores open?
6. What time _____ it?

C. Match each sentence in Column A with a sentence that has the same meaning in Column B. (2 points each)

Column A

___d___ 1. I always get up early.

_____ 2. I always keep my seat belt on.

_____ 3. I never go to bed before midnight.

_____ 4. I usually take a shower before breakfast.

Column B

a. I like to stay up late.

b. I use my seat belt at all times.

c. I take a shower first; then, I have breakfast.

d. I wake up at 5 A.M. every day.

Vocabulary

D. Write the times in words. (2 points each)

1. 9:45 _It's a quarter to ten._
2. 8:50 _____
3. 4:30 _____
4. 12:25 _____

E. Find the eight money words hidden in the puzzle. (2 points each)

D	L	E	K	C	I	N	Q	M	P
C	O	I	O	D	I	M	E	R	E
E	U	L	R	O	L	J	P	N	N
N	B	I	L	L	Y	C	O	I	N
T	V	L	I	A	X	W	E	Z	Y
H	C	Q	U	A	R	T	E	R	G

Communication

F. With a partner, ask and answer questions about your routine after school. Use *first*, *then*, and *after that*. (3 points each)

A: What do you do when you get home from school?

B: First, I eat a snack. Then, I do my homework. After that, I watch TV.

G. Take turns asking and answering the questions. Answer in complete sentences. (3 points each)

1. What time is it?
2. What day is it?
3. What time do you go to bed?
4. What time do you get home from school?

 **SONG**

Mariah Carey

Superstar Mariah Carey, a native of New York, started singing and writing songs as a schoolgirl. She eventually became the number one female soloist in the 1990's. In 2002, Mariah dedicated the song "Hero" to New York City's police officers and fire fighters.

HERO

There's a hero, if you look inside your heart
You don't have to be afraid of what you are
There's an answer, if you reach into your soul
And the sorrow that you know will melt away

Chorus

And then a hero comes along,
with the strength to carry on
And you cast your fears aside,
and you know you can survive
So when you feel like hope is gone,
look inside you and be strong
And you'll finally see the truth
That a hero lies in you

It's a long road when you face the world alone
No one reaches out a hand for you to hold
You can find love if you search within yourself
And the emptiness you felt will disappear

Repeat chorus

Lord knows dreams are hard to follow
But don't let anyone tear them away
Hold on, there will be tomorrow
In time you'll find the way

Repeat chorus

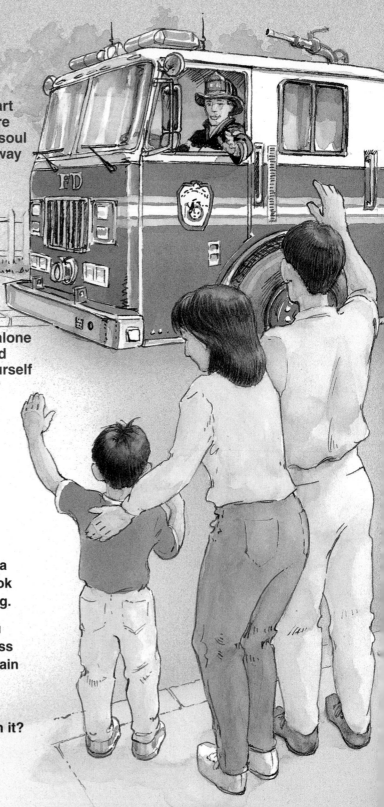

1. 🎧 Read the lyrics to the song. Work with a partner. Select five difficult words and look up their meanings. Then listen to the song.

2. Read the lyrics to the song again. As you listen, underline your favorite part. Discuss your favorite part with a partner and explain why you like it.

3. Discuss with your partner: What is the message in this song? Do you agree with it?

GAME Race Track

You need:

- a coin
- a game piece for yourself (an eraser, etc.)
- one copy of the game board per pair of players

Steps:

1. Flip a coin to decide who goes first and which track the "winner" wants to start on (left or right).
2. Begin at "Start" and flip the coin. For heads, you move one space, for tails two.
3. Follow the rules in the key: make questions, make sentences, go back, or go forward. If you make a mistake, go back one space.
4. Then it's the next person's turn.
5. The first person to cross the finish line wins.

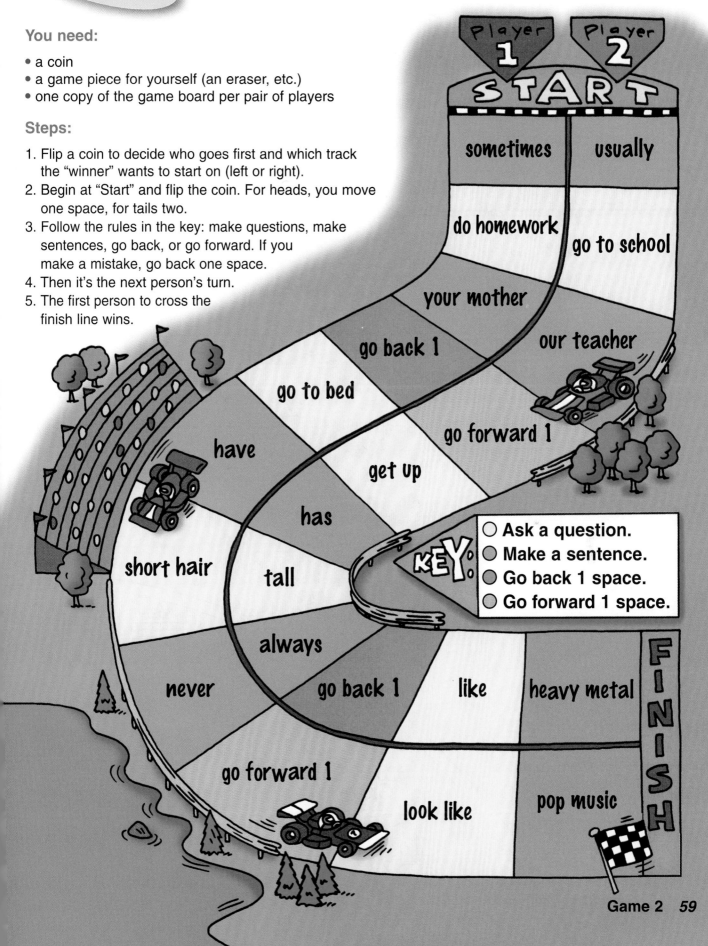

Player 1   Player 2

START

| sometimes | usually |

do homework

go to school

your mother

our teacher

go back 1

go to bed

go forward 1

have

get up

has

short hair   tall

KEY:
○ Ask a question.
● Make a sentence.
● Go back 1 space.
○ Go forward 1 space.

always

never   go back 1   like   heavy metal

FINISH

go forward 1

look like   pop music

Miami—A great place to be!

Learning Goals

Communication
Ask and say where places are
Talk about leisure-time activities
Make and respond to suggestions: *Let's*

Grammar
Prepositions of location
There is/There are

Vocabulary
Places in town
Leisure-time activities

1 Reading

Read the brochure below. Why is Miami a tourist's paradise?

For many travelers, Miami, Florida, is a tourist's paradise. It has sandy white beaches and warm, sunny weather. English and Spanish are the major languages spoken in the area.

There are many exciting attractions in Miami for tourists of all ages, including the Seaquarium, the Planetarium, the Venetian Pool, the Vizcaya Museum and Gardens, and many beautiful parks. And how about a leisurely day on the beach? At the beach, tourists can relax in the sun or go for a swim in the ocean or bay.

South of Miami, in Coral Gables, is the popular Coconut Grove where tourists can find beautiful architecture, theaters, museums, shops, dance clubs, and fabulous restaurants.

Now let's find out more about Miami. Let's start by studying the map.

Coral Gables

⑨

Coconut Grove

⑩ ⑪

Highway 1

⑤
⑥
⑦
⑧

27th Avenue

⑫

Bayshore Drive

Biscayne Bay

Key

1. Crandon Park
2. Lipton Tennis Club
3. School of Marine Biology
4. Seaquarium
5. Museum of Science/Planetarium
6. Madonna's house
7. Vizcaya Museum and Gardens
8. The Chart House Restaurant
9. Venetian Pool
10. Coco Walk
11. Mayfair Stores
12. Dinner Key Marina

Venetian Causeway

Hibiscus Island

Palm Island

Star Island

McArthur Causeway

Port of Miami

South Beach

Fisher Island

Virginia Key

Atlantic Ocean

Crandon Boulevard

Key Biscayne

N
W E
S

2 Communication

Asking about locations

A. 🎧 Listen and read.

1. A: Excuse me. Where's Vizcaya Museum?
   B: It's on Bayshore Drive, next to the Chart House Restaurant.

2. A: Excuse me. Where's Coco Walk?
   B: It's in Coconut Grove, across from the Mayfair Stores.

B. Read the dialogues again. Locate the places on the map.

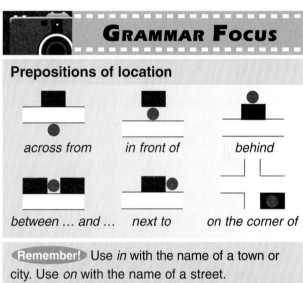

GRAMMAR FOCUS

Prepositions of location

across from   in front of   behind

between ... and ...   next to   on the corner of

Remember! Use *in* with the name of a town or city. Use *on* with the name of a street.
I live **in** New York City.
My house is **on** Prince Street.

3 Practice

In your notebook, write sentences telling where these places are on the map.

1. The Lipton Tennis Club

   It's on Crandon Boulevard, across from Crandon Park.

2. The Chart House Restaurant

3. Vizcaya Museum and Gardens

4. The Seaquarium

5. The Dinner Key Marina

4 Dialogue

🎧 **Listen and read. Circle the word that tells you that Andy likes the Planetarium very much.**

Brian: Andy, is the Venetian Pool just a pool?

Andy: Not really. There are also waterfalls and a restaurant there.

Brian: Where is it?

Andy: It's in Coral Gables. Let's go there on Friday.

Liza: Andy, tell Brian about the Seaquarium.

Andy: Oh, yeah. The Seaquarium is really cool, Brian. You can see killer whales and sharks up close.

Brian: Sounds great!

Andy: And wait until you see the Planetarium and Coconut Grove! The Planetarium is awesome!

Brian: Where is it?

Andy: It's inside the Museum of Science.

Brian: And what about Coconut Grove?

Andy: It's a great place to shop. The restaurants there are wonderful!

Brian: Cool! I can't wait to go to these places.

5 Comprehension

Under each column, write two things that the place has.

Venetian Pool	Seaquarium	Coconut Grove
waterfalls		

6 Vocabulary

Places in towns

🎧 **First, listen and repeat. Then match the places with their descriptions.**

1. bank — a place with lots of stores
2. drugstore ⟍ a place to keep money
3. supermarket — a place to eat
4. museum — a place to buy books
5. post office — a place to see movies
6. movie theater — a place to buy medicine
7. bookstore — a place to wait for buses
8. restaurant — a place to see artwork
9. mall — a place to shop for food
10. bus stop — a place to mail things

GRAMMAR FOCUS

There is/There are

Affirmative statements
There's a supermarket next to the park.
There are many dance clubs in Miami.

Yes/No **questions**
Is there a drugstore in this area?
Are there *any* Caribbean restaurants here?

Negative statements
There isn't a supermarket on this street.
There aren't *any* dance clubs in my town.

Short answers
Yes, **there is**. No, **there isn't**.
Yes, **there are**. No, **there aren't**.

Remember! Use *any* in questions and negative statements.

7 Practice

Look at the map below. Write sentences using *There is, There are, There isn't,* and *There aren't*. Use prepositions in your sentences.

1. drugstore *There is a drugstore behind the*
   post office.

2. banks _____

3. post office _____

4. bookstores _____

5. restaurants _____

8 Practice

Work with a partner. Take turns asking and answering *Yes/No* questions about places on the map.

A: Are there any Asian restaurants in this area?
B: Yes, there are. There's a Korean restaurant on the corner of Miami Avenue and Coral Way.

9 Your Turn

A friend from the United States is coming to visit you. In your notebook, write a letter about interesting places in your town.

Dear_____,
Hi! I'm very excited about your visit to _____.
You'll love it here. There are a lot of wonderful
places in my town...

10 Information Gap

Student A, go to page 91. Student B, go to page 92. Follow the instructions.

11 Listening

🎧 Listen and guess the place. Write the number.

_____ a. Rio de Janeiro, Brazil

_____ b. New York, U.S.A.

_____ c. Beijing, China

13 Communication

Making and responding to suggestions

A. 🎧 Listen to the dialogue.

A: Hey, let's eat out this weekend.
B: Sorry, I can't. I don't have any money.
A: Then let's watch a video at my house.
B: Good idea.

B. Work with a partner. Invite your partner to do one of the activities from Exercise 12A.

14 Listening

🎧 **Read the ads. Then listen to the dialogue. Put a check (✔) next to the correct ad. What do the kids want to do?**

12 Vocabulary

Leisure-time activities

A. Match each picture above with a phrase below. Write the letters before the numbers.

_F_ 1. watch a video or a movie ✔✔

_____ 2. have a party or go to a party _____

_____ 3. hang out with friends _____

_____ 4. visit grandparents _____

_____ 5. eat out _____

_____ 6. go shopping _____

B. Put three checks (✔✔✔) after the activities you _always_ do on weekends; two checks (✔✔) after the ones you _sometimes_ do; and an (✘) after the ones you _never_ do. Compare your results with a classmate.

A Skateboard Contest

🎧 **Work with a partner. Write the missing lines in the dialogue. Choose from the box. Then listen and check your work.**

> What skateboard contest? Hey, wait for me!
> Uh-oh. Andy is in trouble with Caroline.
> No, I don't. Leave me alone.

1 Look, Annie. There's a skateboard contest on Rickenbacker. Let's go.

2 Mom, where are Andy and Brian?

Andy's on the phone with Caroline. And I think Brian is with Joey.

3 I'm sorry, Caroline. I can't come over right now. I have homework. And we still have a guest. Please understand.

4 (1) _____

5 Hey, Andy. Do you want to do something fun?

(2) _____

6 Oh, well. Come on, Liza. The skateboard contest sounds really exciting.

(3) _____

10 What's Brian doing?

1 Dialogue

🎧 **Listen and read. Underline the sentences that show Liza is upset with Andy.**

Liza: Where's Brian?

Andy: He's upstairs in our bedroom, I think.

Liza: What's he doing? Is he reading?

Andy: No, he isn't. He's writing an e-mail.

Liza: Who's he writing to? Is he e-mailing his parents?

Andy: I don't know, Liza. I'm watching TV. Look, do something. Here, read this magazine.

Liza: Gee, Andy. You're grumpy today. I'm out of here.

GRAMMAR FOCUS

Present continuous tense: *be* + verb + *-ing*

Affirmative statements

I	**am**	
He/She	**is**	} playing.
You/We/They	**are**	

Negative statements

I	**am**	
He/She	**is**	} not playing.
You/We/They	**are**	

Yes/No questions

Am I sleeping?

Is { he / she } sleeping?

Are { we / you / they } sleeping?

Affirmative answers

Yes, { I **am**. / he **is**. / she **is**. / we **are**. / you **are**. / they **are**. }

Negative answers

No, { I'm **not**. / he **isn't**. / she **isn't**. / we **aren't**. / you **aren't**. / they **aren't**. }

Remember! Spelling of some present continuous verbs

listen—listen**ing**   play—play**ing**   smile—smil**ing**   sit—sit**ting**

2 Practice

Fill in the blanks with the present continuous form of the verbs.

1. Liza and Andy _are talking_. *(talk)*

2. Brian _____ in the yard. *(sit)*

3. She _____ an e-mail. *(write)*

4. We _____ TV. *(not/watch)*

5. I _____ a bad day. *(have)*

3 Practice

Using the suggested pronouns, write sentences describing the activities in the pictures. Write your sentence on the line below each picture.

do my homework	use a computer
play tennis	take a shower

4 Communication

Work with a classmate. In your notebook, write four *Yes/No* questions about the activities in the pictures in Exercise 3. Then take turns asking and answering your questions.

A: Is the girl in Picture 1 sleeping?
B: No, she isn't. She's doing her homework.

1 *(I)* _____

2 *(They)* _____

3 *(She)* _____

4 *(He)* _____

5 Practice

Fill in the blanks with the present continuous form of the verbs. Use short forms where possible.

| READ | WRITE | DOWNLOADS | WEB |

Hi Mom and Dad. How's everything at home? I *(1. have)* ___I'm having___ a wonderful time here. I *(2. enjoy)* _____ Miami a lot. It's a great place! Why don't you come for a visit? You could meet the Gibson family and see their beautiful house.

The house has four bedrooms. I *(3. write)* _____ this e-mail in Andy's bedroom. I *(4. use)* _____ his computer. The family is downstairs. Mr. and Mrs. Gibson *(5. make)* _____ dinner in the kitchen. Robbie *(6. help)* _____ them. Andy and Liza are in the living room. You're probably wondering why we *(7. not/help)* _____ with dinner. Well, Andy, Liza, and I usually do the dishes after dinner.

I'm attaching a picture of me. I *(8. stand)* _____ in front of the house. Looks great right? I mean the house, not me.

Addresses

Print

Bookmarks

6 Vocabulary

Rooms and parts of the house

🎧 **Listen and repeat. Identify the room or part of the house. Write the number in the circle provided.**

1. basement
2. downstairs
3. upstairs
4. stairs
5. living room
6. dining room
7. bedroom
8. kitchen
9. bathroom
10. garage

7 Your Turn

Draw a picture of your dream house or find a picture of it in a magazine. Write a paragraph describing your dream house or describe your parents' house, including your favorite room in it. Read your paragraph to the class.

8 Reading

A. Read the article twice. The underlined words may be unfamiliar to you. Keep reading and try to guess the meaning of these words from the words around them.

Imagine this <u>scenario</u>. You're entering the <u>gate</u> to your home. You're going up the steps. Then, you stop at the door. You don't have a <u>key</u>. Wait a minute! The door is opening! Who's opening it? No one. It's an <u>automatic</u> door. It's opening because the house <u>recognizes</u> you. Now, your house is welcoming you. Once you're inside, the lights come on, the <u>curtains</u> open up, and your favorite song starts to play. The temperature in the house <u>adjusts</u> to your preferred temperature. The TV screen in the living room lights up. It is telling you that you have phone and e-mail messages! <u>Science fiction</u>? No. It's reality. The house exists, but right now it is only a <u>prototype</u> at Microsoft's Executive Briefing Center in Redmond, Washington.

B. Look up the meanings of the words in Column A. Match the items in Column A with those in Column B.

	A		**B**
1.	_e_ scenario	a.	made-up or untrue story
2.	___ gate	b.	model
3.	___ recognize	c.	truth or true situation
4.	___ curtains	d.	change
5.	___ adjust	e.	situation
6.	___ science fiction	f.	entrance
		g.	window coverings
7.	___ reality	h.	know
8.	___ prototype		

9 Listening

🎧 **The TV screen says that you have two messages. Listen twice and circle the correct answers.**

1. The message 1 caller is at _____.
   (a) the airport (b) home (c) the party

2. According to message 1, the party is on _____.
   (a) Monday (b) Saturday (c) Friday

3. The time of message 2 is _____.
   (a) 4:30 A.M. (b) 5:30 A.M. (c) 4:30 P.M.

4. Austin is caller number 2. He is the _____ of the person he is calling.
   (a) boyfriend (b) brother (c) father

Learn to Learn

Increasing your vocabulary in English

- Read and listen to materials in English.
- When you read, do not let difficult words stop you. Keep reading. Try to guess the meaning of new words from context.
- Use a dictionary.
- Use the new words in sentences.

Progress Check *Units 9 and 10*

Grammar

A. Answer the questions. Use the clues. (2 points each)

1. Where is the post office? *(next to)*
   It's next to the bank.

2. Where is the movie theater? *(between)*

   _____

3. Where is the bank? *(across from)*

   _____

4. Where is the drugstore? *(on the corner of)*

   _____

B. Fill in the blanks with the simple present tense of *be*. (1 point each)

1. There ____is____ a bank next to the park.
2. There _____ (no) any houses in this area.
3. There _____ snacks in the refrigerator.
4. There _____ hot coffee in the kitchen.
5. There _____ (no) any food on the table.

C. Fill in the blanks with the present continuous form of the verbs. (1 point each)

(1. sit) I _'m sitting_ on a bench in the park. It's a nice day. The sun *(2. shine)* _____. Some people *(3. walk)* _____. Some kids *(4. play)* _____ soccer. A man on the grass *(5. read)* _____ a book.

D. Read the answers. Write *Yes/No* questions about the sentences. (2 points each)

1. _Is it raining?_ _____ *(rain)*

   No, it isn't. The sun is shining.

2. _____? *(walk)*

   Yes, they are.

3. _____? *(sleep)*

   No, they aren't. They're relaxing.

4. _____? *(study)*

   No, they aren't. They're playing soccer.

5. _____? *(read)*

   Yes, he is.

6. _____? *(paint)*

   Yes, she is.

Vocabulary

E. Find the eight "house" words in the puzzle. (1 point each)

S	D	M	V	U	B	S	R	T	C	U
R	O	O	B	G	A	R	A	G	E	P
I	D	O	W	N	S	T	A	I	R	S
A	H	R	G	N	E	H	C	T	I	K
T	I	H	A	O	M	E	E	Q	F	I
S	W	T	S	B	E	D	R	O	O	M
P	K	A	L	M	N	H	O	U	S	E
U	B	B	S	O	T	W	R	O	O	A

Communication

F. Write a conversation inviting your partner to do an activity. Use the model below. (3 points each)

A: Hey, let's watch a bike race at the park this weekend.

B: Good idea. But where's the park?

A: It's across from the hospital.

1 Reading

A. Read the article "Homework" on the right. Underline the things that Molly does after school.

B. Match each school subject with the homework assignment.

_d_ 1. English	a.	the life stages of butterflies
____ 2. geography	b.	fractions and decimals
____ 3. science	c.	countries in Europe
____ 4. math	d.	book report on Anne Frank

2 Speaking

With a partner, answer the following:

1. Give one reason why homework is important.
2. Suggest two ways to manage both your school work and other activities.

3 Writing

In your notebook, make a list of all the homework you have on a typical day. Write how much time you spend on each assignment. How much time do you spend doing homework each day?

4 Listening

A. 🎧 Listen twice. Number the following activities according to the sequence Samantha does them.

_3_ 1. She logs on to the Internet.

____ 2. She asks an online school librarian for help.

____ 3. She e-mails her math test to her teacher.

____ 4. Samantha gets on the school bus.

____ 5. She takes her math test.

____ 6. She turns on her laptop computer.

B. Discuss the following as a class:

1. What are two advantages of the Internet?
2. Would you like to be able to study from home, using the Internet to connect to your school? Mention one advantage and one disadvantage of studying from home via the Internet.

Homework

In the United States, homework is getting a lot of attention. Parents think that their kids are too busy, are not getting enough sleep, and are under a lot of stress.

Molly is a sixth grader in San Francisco, California. Read about her typical day.

It is 3:30 Tuesday afternoon. Molly is getting off the school bus. She enters the house and walks straight to her room. She turns on her computer and starts to write her book report on <u>The Diary of Anne Frank</u>.

It is now four o'clock, and Molly is still typing. Thirty minutes later, she stands up and takes her book report to her mom. Her mom reads it, while Molly eats a snack.

You think that Molly can now sit back, talk to friends on the phone, or watch TV, right? Wrong. After her snack, she does her math homework on fractions and decimals. Next comes the geography homework. Today, she's labeling all the countries on a map of Europe. After that, she studies the life stages of butterflies for her science test tomorrow.

It is now 6:00. Molly is practicing piano. At 7:00, she has a quick dinner. After dinner, she reads her book report again. Finally, at 10:00, she goes to bed. Tomorrow is another busy day for Molly.

Many observers say that kids in the United States do not have a lot of time to play and just be kids. There are soccer and baseball practices, ballet and piano lessons, karate, and swimming. For some children, there are extra lessons in English and math outside school. And the list goes on.

How about you? How busy are you?

11 Where were you yesterday?

Learning Goals

Communication
Talk about past events
Express approval and disapproval

Grammar
Simple past tense: *be*
Object pronouns

Vocabulary
Common party and fast foods

1 Dialogue

🎧 Scan the dialogue. What kind of party does Andy suggest? Then, listen and read.

Liza: Andy, where's Brian?

Andy: I don't know. He was in the backyard with Dad a few minutes ago.

Liza: Good. Listen, let's have a surprise party for Brian.

Robbie: Yeah, and let's invite Joey because Brian likes her. They were together all day yesterday.

Andy: Don't say that, Robbie. That's not nice. Now, about the party, Liza. When do you want to have it?

Liza: How about on the twenty-sixth?

Andy: The twenty-sixth is good. Hey, how about a costume party? It's almost Halloween.

Liza: Excellent idea, Andy!

Robbie: Can I help? I like Brian, too.

Andy: Sure. Come on. Help me with the menu. And let's ask Caroline to help, too.

2 Comprehension

Read each sentence. Write *True, False,* or *NI (No Information)*.

___True___ 1. Brian was in the backyard.

_____ 2. Liza is looking for Andy.

_____ 3. Liza's mom is at home.

_____ 4. Liza and Andy are planning a birthday party.

_____ 5. The party will be on a weekend.

3 Useful Phrases

🎧 **Listen and repeat. Which of the expressions below express approval? Which ones express disapproval?**

- Don't say that.
- Excellent idea.
- That's not very nice.

GRAMMAR FOCUS

Simple past tense: be

Affirmative statements	Negative statements
I/He/She/It **was** here yesterday.	I/He/She/It **was not** here yesterday.
You/We/They **were** here yesterday.	You/We/They **were not** here yesterday.

Remember! **Past-time markers**

yesterday: I wasn't home **yesterday** afternoon.

last: They were in Hong Kong **last** summer.

ago: You were very busy a month **ago**.

Short forms (contractions)

was not = wasn't   were not = weren't

4 Practice

Fill in the blanks with *was* or *were*.

1. Brian ___was___ with Joey yesterday.
2. Liza _____ home all day yesterday.
3. Brian and Andy _____ at the gym last Friday.
4. The keys _____ in my bag this morning.
5. Dad _____ in the kitchen a while ago.
6. The Gibsons _____ at a party last night.

5 Practice

In your notebook, write two sentences about each picture on the left. The first sentence should be negative; the second affirmative.

at the movies	at the sports center
at home at a restaurant	at a party

Tom wasn't at home last weekend.

He was at a party.

Tom

Darren and Amy

Jason

Paul

Tara and Tina

GRAMMAR FOCUS

Simple past tense: *be*

Yes/No questions
Was he/she/it here last night?
Were we/they/you here last night?

Information questions with *be*
Who **was** that man with you last night?
Where **were** you yesterday?
Why **were** they absent this morning?
When **was** the exam?

Affirmative answers
Yes, he/she/it **was**.
Yes, we/they/you **were**.

Possible answers
He **was** my classmate 10 years ago.
I **was** at a football game.
Because they **were** sick.
It **was** yesterday.

Negative answers
No, he/she/it **wasn't**.
No, we/they/you **weren't**.

6 Practice

A. Read the dialogue. Underline the words that describe the robber.

Julie: You won't believe this. There was a robbery at our school and I was there!

Josh: Really? When was the robbery?

Julie: Last night between 7 and 9 P.M. Donna and I were in the library across from the computer lab. We saw a man go into the lab. He was short and heavy. His hair was medium length. I think it was red. He was about 30 years old. Maybe he was the robber!

B. Work with a partner. Take turns asking and answering *Yes/No* questions about the story. Use the cues below.

A: Was the man heavy?
B: Yes, he was.

1. heavy
2. hair/long
3. tall
4. library
5. at school between 7 and 9 P.M.

C. In your notebook, write information questions you could ask Julie. Ask about:

1. the man's age
   How old was the man?
2. the time of the robbery
3. the place of the robbery
4. the girls' location at the time of the robbery

7 Your Turn

Work with a partner. Ask and answer these questions. Follow the examples.

A: Were you home at six last night?
B: No, I wasn't.
A: Where were you?
B: I was at a friend's house.

1. Were your parents home at seven last night?
2. Was your dad at work last weekend?
3. Were you at the movies last night?
4. Ask your own question.

Subject pronouns	Object pronouns	Examples	
I	me		me.
he	him		him.
she	her		her.
it	it	Brian knows	it.
you	you		you.
we	us		us.
they	them		them.

9 Practice

A. Replace the underlined words with object pronouns.

1. Robbie likes Brian. He'll miss ___*him*___.

2. Robbie and Andy are preparing the menu. Caroline is helping _____.

3. Ice cream is delicious. I love _____.

4. Joey is Brian's friend. Brian likes _____.

5. Annie and I are going to the party. Would you like to join _____?

6. I can't lift this box. Can you help _____?

B. Compete with a classmate. Circle the object pronouns in the dialogue in Exercise 8. The person who finds the most object pronouns wins.

8 Dialogue

🎧 **Listen and read. Why does Caroline say, "This one's for Brian, not for you."?**

Caroline: Hello?

Andy: Hello. Is this Caroline?

Caroline: Hi, Andy. This is Caroline. Wow, you're calling me! This must be important.

Andy: Well, it is. We're planning a Halloween costume party for Brian.

Caroline: A costume party! OK. So what do you want from me?

Andy: I need your help with the menu. Right now, Liza and Mom are preparing the decorations. Joey's looking for costumes. Her mom's helping her. Robbie and I are planning the menu. Can you help us with it? Please?

Caroline: Hmm. Can I think about it?

Andy: Please, Caroline?

Caroline: Oh, OK. But this one's for Brian, not for you.

Andy: Thanks, Caroline. You're great! See you later.

10 Vocabulary

Match the words with the pictures.

_H_ 1. hamburgers

____ 2. ice cream

____ 3. water

____ 4. chips and salsa

____ 5. hot dogs

____ 6. cake

____ 7. soda

____ 8. spaghetti

____ 9. juice

____ 10. vegetable salad

____ 11. roast chicken

____ 12. apple pie

11 Reading

Read the note. Then write the word the object pronoun refers to.

Andy,

1. I ordered the cake and the apple pie from
2. the Sweet Haven Bakeshop last night.
3. Please pick them up on Saturday morning.
4. After that, help me prepare the salsa. Mom
5. wants to prepare it for us, but salsa is easy
6. to make. So, I asked her to do the roast
7. chicken and the pasta. On Friday, go to
8. the supermarket with Robbie. I have
9. the list of things for you to buy.

Caroline

1. _them_ in line 3 _____

2. _me_ in line 4 _____

3. _it_ in line 5 _____

4. _us_ in line 5 _____

5. _her_ in line 6 _____

6. _you_ in line 9 _____

12 Listening

A. ◠ Listen to the message twice and complete the missing information.

Andy,

_____ called at _____ this afternoon.

She wants you to buy _____ , _____ , and _____ when you go to the supermarket. Call her back.

Her _____ number is_____ .

Mom

B. ◠ Listen again and check your work.

13 Speaking

Talking about where someone was

◠ Listen and repeat. Then role-play the conversation.

A: Were you home last night?

B: No, I wasn't.

A: Where were you?

B: I was at the library.

A: You were at the library on Friday night?

At the Costume Party

A. 🎧 First, look at the pictures. Can you identify some of the costumes? Then, listen and read.

1
Liza, what's the matter? Are you all right?

You know what's wrong, Joey. I know you and Brian like each other.

2
Don't be silly, Liza. Brian and I are just good friends.

Are you sure? You were out with him all day yesterday.

3
Well, yeah. We were out shopping.

Listen, Liza. You're wrong about Brian and me.

See what I mean?

Oh, no! Brian was right there. He knows everything now.

4
Robin Hood! Zorro! Juliet! Come on. They're announcing the winner for best costume.

OK, Superman. We're coming.

5

B. Discuss these questions: Why is Liza worried? What does she think Brian knows?

12 Did you have a good time?

Learning Goals

Communication
Say good-bye
Talk about the past
Talk about occupations

Grammar
The simple past tense: regular and irregular verbs

Vocabulary
Occupations

1 Dialogue

🎧 **Listen and read. Circle Brian's present for Liza.**

Brian: Well, this is it. I can't believe I'm leaving. Time went by fast.

Robbie: Umm, Brian? I have a present for you. It's my favorite baseball.

Joey: And here's something from all of us. It's the family picture you took at the picnic. I hope you like it.

Brian: Gee. Thanks everyone. I had a great time. I really enjoyed my stay here.

Andy: We're glad you came. Good luck!

Brian: Uh, Liza, here's a present for you. It's a bracelet. I bought it last week. Joey helped me.

Liza: Oh, Brian, thank you. It's beautiful. Take care. And keep in touch.

Brian: Sure. Robbie, thanks for the baseball.

Robbie: Bye. Please come back.

2 Comprehension

Cross out the wrong information. Then correct the sentence to make it true.

1. The Gibsons are ~~welcoming~~ *saying good-bye to* Brian.
2. They are at the airport.
3. Robbie gave Brian a video game.
4. Joey gave Brian a painting.
5. Liza helped Brian buy a present.

3 Useful Phrases

 Listen and repeat. Underline the expression that means "Write or call us once in a while."

- Good-bye./Bye.
- Good luck.
- Take care.
- Keep in touch.

GRAMMAR FOCUS

Simple past tense: regular verbs

Affirmative statements		Negative statements		
I He She It You We They	smiled. played. stopped. cried.	I He She It You We They	did not	smile. play. stop. cry.

Remember! For verbs ending in a consonant and *y*, change *y* to *i* and add *–ed*.
For verbs ending in a vowel and *y*, just add *–ed*.

4 Practice

Write the simple past form of the verbs.

1. Liza ___promised___ to write to Brian. (*promise*)
2. Brian and Joey _____ for presents. (*shop*)
3. Brian _____ in Miami. (*stay*)
4. Brian _____ his bags to the car. (*carry*)
5. Joey _____ by to say good-bye. (*stop*)

5 Practice

Change the following into negative sentences. Write the sentences in your notebook.

1. I went to the beach last summer.
   I did not go to the beach last summer.
2. The students studied for their exam.
3. We enjoyed last night's party.
4. She tried hard.
5. They stayed home last weekend.

GRAMMAR FOCUS

Simple past tense of some irregular verbs

be	=	**was, were**	get	=	**got**
come	=	**came**	go	=	**went**
do	=	**did**	read	=	**read**
has	=	**had**	say	=	**said**
leave	=	**left**	take	=	**took**
give	=	**gave**	tell	=	**told**

6 Reading

Read Brian's e-mail. Circle the verbs in the past form.

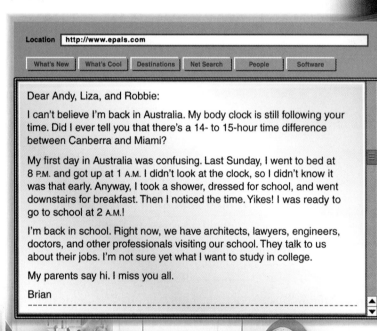

Location   http://www.epals.com

| What's New | What's Cool | Destinations | Net Search | People | Software |

Dear Andy, Liza, and Robbie:

I can't believe I'm back in Australia. My body clock is still following your time. Did I ever tell you that there's a 14- to 15-hour time difference between Canberra and Miami?

My first day in Australia was confusing. Last Sunday, I went to bed at 8 P.M. and got up at 1 A.M. I didn't look at the clock, so I didn't know it was that early. Anyway, I took a shower, dressed for school, and went downstairs for breakfast. Then I noticed the time. Yikes! I was ready to go to school at 2 A.M.!

I'm back in school. Right now, we have architects, lawyers, engineers, doctors, and other professionals visiting our school. They talk to us about their jobs. I'm not sure yet what I want to study in college.

My parents say hi. I miss you all.

Brian

7 Practice

Have a competition. Go to page 90.

8 Practice

First, circle the wrong information. Then rewrite the sentences to make them true.

1. Brian went to (Canada) as an exchange student.
   Brian didn't go to Canada. He went to the United States.

2. Brian went to bed at 9 P.M.
   _____.

3. Brian got up very late.
   _____.

4. Brian took a shower at eight in the morning.
   _____.

5. Brian went downstairs for dinner.
   _____.

GRAMMAR FOCUS

Yes/No questions		Affirmative answers		Negative answers	
Did	I he she it you we they	**smile?** **stop?** **play?** **cry?**	Yes,	I he she it you we they	**did.**

Negative answers: No, I / he / she / it / you / we / they **didn't.**

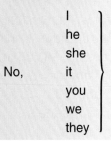

9 Practice

Work with a partner. Ask and answer the questions orally. If the answer is *no*, give the correct information.

1. Did you go to the movies last weekend?
   No, I didn't. I went to a dance club.

2. Did you have breakfast this morning?
3. Did a classmate call you last night?
4. Did your parents stay home last weekend?
5. Did you and your family watch TV last night?

10 Practice

Work with a partner. Read the dialogue on page 80 again. In your notebook, write four *Yes/No* questions. Take turns asking and answering your questions.

Did Brian go back to Australia?

11 Vocabulary

A. Read Brian's e-mail on page 82 again. Circle all the occupations he mentions.

B. Match each occupation with the correct picture. Write the letter.

_F_	1. doctor	____	6. nurse
____	2. salesperson	____	7. mail carrier
____	3. police officer	____	8. teacher
____	4. accountant	____	9. computer programmer
____	5. architect	____	10. carpenter

12 Practice

Have a competition! Go to page 90.

COOL JOBS FOR TEENAGERS

Video-game girl

Would you like to play a lot of video games and get paid for it? Impossible? Not if you're Diane Park. At 13, Diane worked for a research company in Lansing, Michigan. She tested video games. Diane decided what she liked and didn't like about the games. The video-game maker used Diane's suggestions to improve the products.

Diane enjoyed her job. She said, "I got paid for doing something fun!"

Ball wonder

Chris Turner is 16 years old. He had a cool job last summer. Chris worked as a ball boy at the U.S. Open Tennis Tournament in New York. He provided fresh tennis balls, water, and towels for the tennis players.

Why was it cool to work as a ball boy at the U.S. Open? Chris met the world's best tennis players there, including Anna Kournikova, the Williams sisters, and Pete Sampras. He had a lot of fun and made $550 for 80 hours of picking up tennis balls. And, of course, Chris got to be on TV! Pretty cool job!

13 Reading

Answer these questions in complete sentences.

1. What was Diane Park's job when she was 13?

   Diane was a video-game tester.

2. Did Diane enjoy her job? Why?
   _____
   _____

3. As a ball boy, what did Chris do at the U.S. Open Tennis Tournament?
   _____

4. Did Chris enjoy his summer job? Give two reasons.
   _____
   _____

14 Speaking

In your notebook, write five *Yes/No* questions about the articles. With a partner, take turns asking and answering your questions.

A: Did Diane get paid for playing video games?
B: Yes, she did.

15 Your Turn

Work with a partner. Tell each other what you did last summer.

84 Unit 12

Progress Check *Units 11 and 12*

Grammar

A. Circle the correct pronoun. Draw a line through the incorrect one. (1 point each)

1. I don't want any chips. Do you want (~~they~~ them)?
2. Mark and (I, me) were good friends in middle school.
3. The teacher helped (we, us) with math.
4. David talked to (she, her) about the party.
5. (She, Her) is in Canada.
6. You asked (he, him) a question.

B. Write the past tense forms of the verbs. (1 point each)

1. say ___said___
2. start _____
3. take _____
4. jog _____
5. make _____
6. be _____
7. like _____
8. tell _____
9. wash _____
10. cry _____

C. Fill in the blanks with the simple past forms of the verbs. (1 point each)

1. The car ___stopped___ (stop) at the corner.
2. I _____ (study) until 10 P.M. last night.
3. Dad _____ (read) the newspaper.
4. They _____ (have) a busy day.
5. Mom _____ (wake) me up early.
6. We _____ (visit) our friends last week.

D. Make the verbs negative. (3 points each)

1. They went to France.
   They didn't go to France.

2. I bought a present for my sister.
   _____

3. We were home yesterday.
   _____

4. The car was in the garage.
   _____

E. Change the sentences in Exercise D to *Yes/No* questions. (3 points each)

1. *Did they go to France?*_____
2. _____
3. _____
4. _____

Vocabulary

F. Cross out the word that does not belong. (1 point each)

1. cake   ~~soda~~   ice cream   pie
2. hot dogs   hamburgers   salad   beef chili
3. salsa   juice   coffee   water

G. Match each occupation with its definition. (1 point each)

carpenter	nurse	mail carrier
police officer	architect	teacher

___teacher___ 1. works in schools

_____ 2. helps keep peace and order

_____ 3. designs houses and buildings

_____ 4. assists doctors and takes care of patients

_____ 5. delivers mail and packages

_____ 6. builds houses

Communication

H. Work with a partner. Ask each other about your weekend. (6 points each)

A: How was your weekend?
B: It was great!
A: What did you do?
B: I went to a party on Saturday. On Sunday, I was at a soccer game.

SONG

Evan and Jaron

Evan and Jaron Lowenstein are brothers from Atlanta, Georgia, in the United States. When they were very young they wanted to become baseball players! But luckily they also loved to write songs. The hit song "Crazy for This Girl" is on their album "Outerspace."

Crazy For This Girl

She rolls the window down
And she talks over the sound
Of the cars that pass us by
And I don't know why
But she's changed my mind

Chorus

Would you look at her
She looks at me
She's got me thinking about her constantly
But she don't know how I feel
And as she carries on without a doubt
I wonder if she's figured out
I'm crazy for this girl

She was the one to hold me
The night the sky fell down
And what was I thinking when
The world didn't end
Why didn't I know what I know now

Repeat chorus

And right now, face to face, all my fears pushed aside
And right now I'm ready to spend the rest of my life with you

Repeat chorus

1. 🎧 Read and listen to the song. What does the phrase "I'm crazy for this girl" mean?

2. Read the lyrics again. Underline the line that breaks a grammar rule from Unit 5. (Hint: check the Grammar boxes!)

3. Discuss with a partner: How does this song make you feel?

GAME Add Up the Questions

You need:
- a die, or write the numbers 1-6 on pieces of paper and fold them up
- one copy of the game board per pair or group

Steps:
1. Work in pairs or small groups.
2. Player A reads the first sentence aloud. (For example, *Danny ate dinner in his apartment on Friday.*) Player A then rolls the die or picks a number. If the number is 1, 2, 3, or 4, player A asks a question using the *wh-* word in that box.
   Example: Player A (picks a 1): **Who ate dinner in his apartment on Friday?**
3. If player A answers the question correctly, he or she gets a point.
4. If a player rolls a 5, he or she gets one free point. If a player rolls a 6, he or she loses one point.
5. The first player to get five points is the winner.

Ask **Who** Ask **What** Ask **Where** Ask **When** **+ 1 point** **− 1 point**

1 Danny ate dinner in his apartment on Friday.

2 Ricardo rode on a roller coaster on Saturday.

3 Billy bought a bull dog at Buster's Pet Store last April.

4 Sigmund saw a snail in the sandbox on Sunday.

5 Haley helped a horse up a hill this morning.

6 Penny put a present under the tree at midnight.

Fun with Grammar

Unit 2, 6 Practice, page 12

For the teacher: Divide the class into teams. Choose one representative from each team (a "team rep"). The teacher tells the team rep where to put an object. The first team rep to do the action correctly gets a point for his or her team. Change team reps and repeat the activity.

Suggested commands:

1. Put your English book **under** your desk.
2. Put your pencil case **in** your backpack.
3. Put your pen **above** your head.
4. Put your English notebook **on** the floor.
5. Put your eraser **in** your pencil case.
6. Put your English book **above** your head.
7. Sit **on** the floor.
8. Write your name **on** the cover of your notebook.
9. Put your pen **in** your notebook.
10. Put your ruler **under** your pencil case.

Unit 3, 3B Practice, page 19

For the teacher: Allow 40 seconds for students to complete the list.

For the students: Work as fast as you can. The student who gets the most correct answers in 40 seconds wins. Write the plural of each word in the list.

Singular	Plural	Singular	Plural
1. sentence	_____	11. day	_____
2. city	_____	12. place	_____
3. language	_____	13. child	_____
4. man	_____	14. foot	_____
5. class	_____	15. woman	_____
6. baby	_____	16. tooth	_____
7. teacher	_____	17. dictionary	_____
8. box	_____	18. boy	_____
9. pencil	_____	19. sandwich	_____
10. page	_____	20. lady	_____

Unit 3, 9B Practice, page 21

For the teacher: Divide the class into two teams. Give each team either List A or List B below. The student on each team who gets the list first writes *a* or *an* in the blank next to the first noun. That student then passes the list to the next student, who answers the next item and checks the first student's answer. The first team to finish the entire list correctly wins.

List A	List B
1. _____ woman	1. _____ article
2. _____ boy	2. _____ banana
3. _____ apple	3. _____ computer
4. _____ answer	4. _____ animal
5. _____ banana	5. _____ woman
6. _____ computer	6. _____ apartment
7. _____ old man	7. _____ student
8. _____ doctor	8. _____ person
9. _____ article	9. _____ box
10. _____ office	10. _____ umbrella
11. _____ person	11. _____ apple
12. _____ animal	12. _____ answer
13. _____ umbrella	13. _____ doctor
14. _____ student	14. _____ office
15. _____ apartment	15. _____ old man

Unit 4, 9 Practice, page 26

For the teacher: Make sure that the students are seated in rows. Assign ordinal numbers for each row; for example, row 1 is the first row. Then have the students in each row count off, each row beginning with number 1. Give a command to a student from any row, using ordinals to identify the student. For example: *The sixth student in the first row, raise your hand.* If the student responds quickly and correctly, he or she earns a point for the team.

Unit 4, 11 Practice, page 27

For the teacher: Divide the class into two teams. Write an answer on the board *(My husband is at work.)*. Have the students write a question for the answer (*Where's your husband?*). Call on one student from Team A. If that student gives the correct question, Team A gets a point. Continue the game, this time calling a student from Team B. Write the following suggested answers on the board one at a time.

Suggested answers:

1. My children are in school.
2. I'm _____ years old.
     (your age)
3. My birthday is on _____.
     (your birthday)
4. My shoes are under the table
5. Today is _____.
     (today's date)
6. My name is _____.
     (your name)
7. My address is _____.
     (your address)
8. The English test is on _____.
     (day of test)
9. My telephone number is _____.
     (your telephone number)
10. My husband's name is _____.
     (your husband's name)

Fun with Grammar

Unit 5, 4 Practice, page 33

For the teacher: Form teams of three members each. Draw a Tic-Tac-Toe grid on the board. Have the students play Tic-Tac-Toe. Say the name of a member of Andy's family. Each team will write three sentences about that family member. The team who writes three correct sentences goes to the board and fills in a box in the Tic-Tac-Toe grid.

Teacher: Robbie.
Team 3:   Robbie is Gloria's son. He's Liza's brother. He's Martha's grandson.

Unit 12, 7 Practice, page 82

For the teacher: Follow the instructions.

1. Divide the class into two teams. Give list A to Team A; list B to Team B. Tell students to memorize the simple past forms of the verbs. After three minutes, take the lists away.
2. On the board, make two lists of the base forms of some of the verbs. Each list should have the same verbs arranged in different order.
3. Have a representative from each team go to the board and choose any verb to write in the past form.
4. Each student should write only one verb, but he or she may correct the previous student's answer. The first team to give all the correct answers wins.

List A	List B
1. write = **wrote**	1. drink = **drank**
2. think = **thought**	2. say = **said**
3. come = **came**	3. read = **read**
4. do = **did**	4. think = **thought**
5. eat = **ate**	5. get = **got**
6. buy = **bought**	6. come = **came**
7. go = **went**	7. do = **did**
8. take = **took**	8. go = **went**
9. drink = **drank**	9. buy = **bought**
10. get = **got**	10. eat = **ate**
11. read = **read**	11. write = **wrote**
12. say = **said**	12. take = **took**

Unit 12, 12 Practice, page 83

For the teacher: Follow the instructions below.

1. Prepare a list of ten occupations.
2. Divide the class into small groups (3–4 students).
3. Have a representative from each group come to the front of the class.
4. Show the representatives the occupation on the top of the list.
5. The representatives go back to their groups and draw a picture of the word.
6. The team that guesses the occupation gets a point.

Information Gaps

Unit 7, 6 Information Gap, page 47

1. **Ask Student B when you have the following classes. Write each class in your schedule.**

| science   music   geography   gym |

A: When is our *science class*?
B: It's *on Mondays and Fridays at nine o'clock*.

2. **Now look at the completed schedule. When can you study together?**

	Monday	Tuesday	Wednesday	Thursday	Friday
9:00	science	math	English	math	science
10:00			English		
11:00		history		art	history
12:00	LUNCH	LUNCH	LUNCH	LUNCH	LUNCH

Unit 9, 10 Information Gap, page 63

You and Student B have the same maps, but with different information. Take turns asking and giving information about the location of these places on the map. Write the places on your map in the correct location.

| park   public pool   bank |
| mall   post office   art museum |

A: Is there a *mall* on the map?
B: Yes, there is. It's *across from* the *bus stop*.

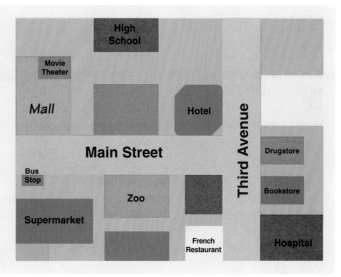

Information Gaps

Unit 7, 6 Information Gap, page 47

1. **Ask Student A when you have the following classes. Write each class in the schedule.**

| math   English   history   art |

B: When is our *math class*?
A: It's *on Tuesdays and Thursdays at nine o'clock.*

2. **Now look at the completed schedule. When can you study together?**

	Monday	Tuesday	Wednesday	Thursday	Friday
9:00	science				science
10:00	geography	music		music	geography
11:00			gym		
12:00	LUNCH	LUNCH	LUNCH	LUNCH	LUNCH

Unit 9, 10 Information Gap, page 63

You and Student A have the same maps, but with different information. Take turns asking and giving information about the location of these places on the map. Write the places on your map in the correct location.

| zoo   high school   movie theater |
| hotel   drugstore   hospital |

B: Is there a *zoo* on the map?
A: Yes, there is. It's *next to* the *bus stop.*

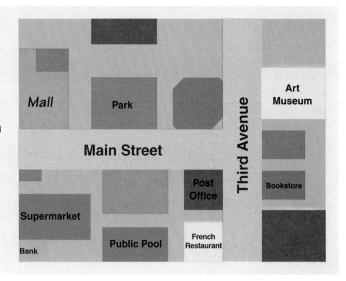

Project 1 A Snapshot of Me

Write four paragraphs about yourself and your interests. Find a photograph or an illustration for each paragraph. Use Sara's project below to help you. Talk about your project to your class or group.

1. Introduce yourself.

Hi! My name is Sara Jones. I'm 12 years old. This is a picture of me and my cat. My cat's name is Henry.

2. Write about where you live.

I live in Plano. It's a suburb of Dallas in Texas. It's a big town and there's a lot to do. I really like it.

3. Write about your school and your classes.

I'm in the seventh grade at Carpenter Middle School. My favorite subjects are math and gym. I don't like art. It's boring.

4. Write about your favorite singer, athlete, movie star, or TV star.

I like different sports. My favorite sport is soccer. My favorite soccer player is Ronaldo. He's from Brazil and he's a fabulous player.

Project 2 A Snapshot of My Family

Write paragraphs about your family members. Bring photographs of your family to show your class. Use the project below to help you. Then, tell your class about your family.

1. Write about your mom.

My mom's name is Ellen. She's a lawyer. She works in the city. But on the weekends, she spends time with me. She likes to paint. She paints pictures of her family and friends. She has a lot of friends.

2. Write about your dad.

My dad's name is Mark. He's a real-estate agent. He sells houses. He usually works at home, and he works on the computer a lot. He's very interested in computers and the Internet. He also likes gardening. He has a vegetable garden in the backyard. We spend a lot of time together in the garden.

3. Write about another member of your family.

This is my big brother. His name's Ben and he's in college. He goes to the University of California in Los Angeles. He studies filmmaking. He has a really pretty girlfriend named Maha. I miss him. I'm happy when he comes home for holidays.

4. Write about another member of your family.

We have a dog named Alfred. He's an English bulldog, and he's four years old. He's pretty lazy. He likes to sleep on our living-room sofa. He sleeps about 20 hours a day. He snores a lot.

Project 3   A Snapshot of My Town

Make a tourist brochure of things to do in and around your city. Paste photos that show these places. Use the guide about Washington, D.C. below to help you.

1. Write about interesting places to go in your city.

There are many things to do in Washington, D.C. You can visit museums such as the Air and Space Museum. It is awesome. From the museums, you can walk to the Washington Monument. You can also visit the Capitol and the White House, where the president lives and works.

2. Write about a good place to go shopping.

The best place to go shopping in Washington is Pentagon City. It's a huge mall. The Wall is a store there. It is a great place to buy CDs and video games. There's also a food court with many different restaurants. Lots of people go to Pentagon City on weekends.

3. Write about a good place to eat.

Chipotle is a fun place to eat. They serve great Mexican food. They have excellent burritos. The burritos are really big, but pretty cheap! The guacamole there is very good, too.

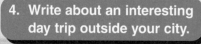

4. Write about an interesting day trip outside your city.

SixFlags

Six Flags America is about 30 minutes from Washington, DC. It is a big amusement park with lots of great rides. Six Flags has Batwing, a hanging roller-coaster. It's awesome! And there's the Superman Ride of Steel. You go up about 250 feet, then go straight down! It's really scary.

Names, addresses, and phone numbers

Here are some examples of how people in the United States address envelopes.

G. Rodriguez
Mexico 1003
Buenos Aires 1097, AR

Argentina

Mr. and Mrs. Robert Stewart
603 Willow Ave.
Denver, CO 80202
U.S.A.

AERO POSTALE

Factfile

ADDRESSING LETTER ENVELOPES

Abbreviations

Street and building names

Street = St.	Avenue = Ave.
Boulevard = Blvd.	Road = Rd.
Apartment = Apt.	Post Office = P.O.

Some U.S. state names

New York = NY	California = CA
Florida = FL	Colorado = CO
District of Columbia = DC	

Special telephone numbers in the United States

Emergency: 911
Directory Assistance: 411
Toll-free Number:
1-800 or 1-888

Koju Doi
2122 California St.
Washington, DC 20008

Washington Women
USA

Ms. Sandra Carter
288 Hudson St. Apt. 5122
New York, NY 10016

AIR MAIL

Margarita Perez
Avenida de Aragon 4
Valencia 46021, Spain

Espaテ。

Mr. Tom D. Mizoi
288 Bay Blvd.
San Diego, CA 92105
U.S.A.

AERO POSTALE

1 Comprehension

Look at the letters and answer the questions.

1. What abbreviation do you use to address a letter to a married couple? _____Mr. and Mrs._____

2. What abbreviation do you use for a man? _____ For a woman? _____

3. What is Tom's last name? _____ His middle initial? _____

4. What is Sandra's last name? _____

5. What is the number of Sandra's apartment? _____

6. What street do Mr. and Mrs. Stewart live on? _____

7. What is the zip code in San Diego, California? _____

2 Comparing Cultures

Work with a partner. Discuss the questions below.

1. Compare the formats used on the envelopes with the format used in your country. What are the same? What are different?

2. What are some abbreviations you use on letters?

3. What are some emergency phone numbers in your country?

3 Your Turn

Address a letter to Andy using the information below. Use abbreviations when possible. Write your address on the upper left-hand corner of the envelope.

Name: Andy Gibson

Address: 55 Isabel Street

City: Coral Gables

State: Florida

Country: United States of America

Zip Code: 33134

AIR MAIL

All about Australia

My country, Australia, is the only country that's a continent. It's in the Southern Hemisphere. Most Australians live in big cities near the ocean. The middle of the country, the Outback, is dry and dusty. Not many people live there.

There are lots of fun things to do in Australia. In the Outback, you can visit Ayers Rock. It's a very, very big red rock—it's 345 meters tall and 3 kilometers wide! You can climb to the top in about 3 hours. In southeastern Australia, you can visit Sydney, a very big and exciting city. The weather in Sydney is usually sunny and warm, and Sydney has great beaches. Sydney's most famous landmark is the Opera House. In northeastern Australia, you can visit the Great Barrier Reef. You can stay on beautiful islands near the reef, then take snorkeling or diving trips to see the cool fish. But watch out for sharks!

Australian English has lots of interesting words. We call our country Oz, and we call ourselves Aussies. When we see our friends, we say g'day (good day) instead of hello. For barbecues we say barbies, for presents we say prezzies, and for kangaroos we say roos.

Speaking of roos, Australia has lots of them. We have over 40 different kinds of kangaroos. Kangaroos carry their babies in a pouch. When a little roo is frightened, it jumps headfirst into the pouch. We also have koalas. Koalas live in eucalyptus trees and eat eucalyptus leaves. Another common animal is the wombat. Wombats look like baby bears. They live underground.

①

②

1 Comprehension

A. Identify each picture below.

1. ___Koala___   2._____   3._____

4. _____   5._____   6._____

B. Fill in the blanks.

1. Australia isn't an island, it's a ___continent___.

2. Not many people live in the _____ because it's dry and dusty.

3. a. *Oz* means _____.

   b. *Roos* means _____.

   c. *Prezzies* means _____.

   d. *Aussies* means _____.

   e. *G'day* means _____.

   f. *Barbies* means _____.

4. A baby kangaroo jumps in his parent's _____ when he's frightened.

5. Koalas eat _____ leaves.

2 Comparing Cultures

Work in groups of five. Discuss the questions below. Share the results with the class.

1. What are some places to visit in your country?
2. What are some animals in your country?
3. What are some English-based words and expressions in your country?

3 Your Turn

Write a paragraph about one of the topics below. Share your paragraph with your classmates. Use Brian's description of his country as a model.

1. Facts about your country
2. Interesting places to visit in your country
3. Interesting animals in your country

American Festivals and Holidays

Like people all over the world, Americans love to celebrate festivals and holidays. Halloween, Thanksgiving, St. Patrick's Day, and Independence Day are special holidays in the United States.

Halloween (October 31st)

On Halloween, people decorate their houses with jack-o'-lanterns. Jack-o'-lanterns are orange pumpkins with faces cut out of them and a light put inside. At night, children and teenagers dress in costumes and go to houses in their neighborhoods. When a neighbor comes to the door, the kids say *Trick or treat!* This means the neighbor should give them a treat or the kids may play a trick. Of course, the neighbors give candy to the kids. Kids have a lot of candy when they get home!

Thanksgiving (Fourth Thursday in November)

In the 1600s, some people left England to have religious freedom. These people were called Pilgrims. They settled in North America. Their first year in America was hard; many died. The Native Americans helped them grow corn and other vegetables. In 1621, the Pilgrims had a big feast to thank their Native American friends. That was the first Thanksgiving. In America today, Thanksgiving is one of the biggest holidays of the year. Families gather together for traditional Thanksgiving foods such as turkey, sweet potatoes, and pumpkin pie. People give thanks to family, friends, and God for their good fortune.

St. Patrick's Day (March 17th)

St. Patrick's Day is an Irish-American festival. St. Patrick is the patron saint of Ireland, and green is the color of Ireland. On this day, people wear green clothes, hats, and jewelry. People drink green beer and eat green-colored cakes, cookies, and even green hot dogs. There are lots of parades and parties on St. Patrick's Day. This day celebrates one of America's many different ethnic groups.

Independence Day (July 4th)

On July 4th, Americans celebrate the day America became a country. In the 1700s, the east coast of America was a British colony. Americans fought the British and became independent on July 4, 1776. Today, on the fourth of July, people fly flags and wear red, white, and blue. They watch parades and firework shows, and eat typical American summer food like barbecue, hamburgers, hot dogs, potato salad, and ice cream. Americans are especially proud of their country and their freedom on this day.

1 Comprehension

A. Match the pictures with the holidays.

_____D_____ 1. St. Patrick's Day

_____ 2. Independence Day

_____ 3. Thanksgiving

_____ 4. Halloween

B. Fill in the blanks. Choose from the words in the box.

candy	British	Ireland	turkey
green food	1776	1621	

1. The first Thanksgiving in the United States was in ____1621____.

2. On Thanksgiving, Americans eat _____.

3. On Halloween, kids get _____.

4. On St. Patrick's Day, people eat _____.

5. St. Patrick is the patron saint of _____.

6. Before July 4th, America was a _____ colony.

7. Americans won their independence in _____.

2 Comparing Cultures

What are some special holidays and festivals in your country? Write about them in your notebook.

3 Your Turn

Write a paragraph about your favorite festival or holiday. Share your paragraph with your classmates.

Useful Words and Expressions

UNIT 1

Nouns
airport
classmate
friend
homework
movie star
movies
name
pen pal
present

Adjectives
favorite
old
good-looking
great

Verb
be (am, is, are)

Subject Pronouns
I
You
He
She
It
We
They

Expressions
What's your name?
How old are you?
Excuse me.
Are you … [name]?
Hello.
Welcome to … [name of city].
Nice to meet you.
Who's your favorite
  singer/actor/music group?
How about you?

UNIT 2

Nouns
backpack
bag
beach
CD player
jacket
luggage
passport
sneakers
sunglasses

ticket
trunk
video camera

Verb
be (isn't/aren't)

Prepositions
in
on
above
under
at

Possessive adjectives
my
your
his
her
our
their

Expressions
How are you?
I'm fine, thanks./Fine, thanks.
Let's go.
Where is …? / Where are…?

UNIT 3

Nouns
city
class
country
exchange student
nationality
student

Articles
a
an

Demonstrative Pronouns/
Adjectives
this
that
these
those

Expressions
Where are you from?
I'm sorry.
I'm from [Canada].
Are you [American]?
Look out!

Cool!
I'm kidding.
By the way…
See you later.

UNIT 4

Nouns
address
birthday
date
girlfriend
guest pass
information
month
volunteer

Prepositions
in
on

Question Words
Who
What
What time
How
Where
When

Expressions
What's today's date?
What's your phone number?
What's your last name?
When's your birthday?
Can you spell that, please?
Can you repeat that, please?
Is there anything else?
No, thanks. That's it.
You're welcome.
Sure.
Let me see.

UNIT 5

Nouns
Family relationships
aunt
brother
child/children
cousin
daughter
family
father
grandchild/grandchildren
granddaughter

grandfather
grandmother
grandparents
grandson
mother
parents
sister
son
uncle

Verbs
have
has

Adjectives
blond
blue
brown
pretty
big
happy

Expressions
Do you have any brothers or
  sisters?
What does he or she look like?

UNIT 6

Nouns
Types of music
classical music
heavy metal
hip-hop
opera
pop
rap
rock

Other nouns
ballet
classical music
computer
sports
video games

Adjectives
curly
funny
heavy
long
medium build
medium height
medium length
short
straight
tall
thin
wavy

Verbs
hate
like
love

Expressions
What kind of music do you like?
They're awesome!
Oh, wow! This is great!

UNIT 7

Nouns
U.S. Currency
bill (a dollar bill)
cent
dime
dollar
half dollar
nickel
penny
quarter

Verbs
call
come
enjoy
get
live
open
say
start
wait

Expressions
Oh, all right.
Stop it.
Don't say that.
Don't worry.
What time is it?
What time does the movie start?
Let me get the tickets.
How much are the tickets?
Here you are.
Can I come in?
No, I'm afraid you can't.
May I come in?
Please come in.
It's late.
Good night.

UNIT 8

Nouns
alarm clock
banana
bread and butter
breakfast
bus
car
cereal
coffee
dinner
Internet
juice
lunchtime
routine
rush
track-and-field team

Sequence words
first
then
after that

Verb
Daily routines
brush your teeth
do homework
eat dinner
get dressed
get up
go to bed
go to the gym
have breakfast
leave home
take a shower
take the bus
watch TV

UNIT 9

Nouns
Places in towns
bank
bookstore
bus stop
dance club
drugstore
mall
movie theater
museum
planetarium
post office
restaurant
supermarket
swimming pool
zoo

Useful Words and Expressions

Adjectives
awesome
beautiful
famous
leisurely
popular
rich
wonderful

Expressions
Where is …?
It's …
Let's go there.
Let's eat out.
Good idea.
Yeah! That'd be great.
Sounds great!
Cool. I can't wait to go.

UNIT 10

Verbs
call
enjoy
go
listen
play
read
sit
sleep
smile
stand
study
talk
use
walk
write

Verbs/Activities
do homework
play tennis
read a book
take a shower
use a computer
write an e-mail

Expressions
You're grumpy today.
I'm out of here.
What's he/she doing?
There is … / There are …
Is there …/ Are there …?

UNIT 11

Nouns
backyard
birthday party
costumes
Halloween
library
menu

Object pronouns
me
him
her
it
you
us
them

Verbs
be (was/were; wasn't/weren't)
bring
buy
give
help
order
pick up
prepare

Expressions
a few minutes/a month ago
all day yesterday
last night/weekend/summer/
  month/year
yesterday afternoon
Are you sure?
Can I help?
Listen, let's have a surprise party.
Oh no!
So what?
That's not very nice.
How about a costume party?
Excellent idea!
Where were you?
Don't be silly.

UNIT 12

Verbs
Irregular past tense
be = was/were
come = came
do = did
get = got
give = gave
go =went
have/has = had
leave = left
read = read
say = said
tell = told
take = took

Expressions
Well, this is it.
I had a great time.
Good-bye./Bye.
Good luck.
Take care.
Keep in touch.
Have a great trip.
I miss you.
Please come back.